THE
COSMOLOGY OF THE RIGVEDA,

THE COSMOLOGY OF THE RIGVEDA, AN ESSAY

BY

H. W. WALLIS, M.A.,

GONVILLE AND CAIUS COLLEGE, CAMBRIDGE.

KALPAZ

ISBN: 978-93-5128-797-1(HB)

First Published in 1887
Indian Reprint in 2017

Published by

Kalpaz Publications
C-30, Satyawati Nagar,
Delhi – 110052
E-mail: kalpaz@hotmail.com
Website: kalpazpublications.com
Ph.: +91-9212142040

Cataloging in Publication Data—DK
Courtesy: D.K. Agencies (P) Ltd. <docinfo@dkagencies.com>

Wallis, H. W. (Henry White), 1861-1887, **author.**
The cosmology of the Rigveda : an essay / by H.W. Wallis (M.A.).
pages cm
"First published in 1887"—Title page verso.
ISBN 9789351287971

1. Vedas. R%˜gveda—Criticism, interpretation, etc. 2. Hindu mythology. I. Title.

BL1112.56.W35 2017 DDC 294.5921046 23

PREFACE.

The object of this essay is not so much to present a complete picture of the Cosmology of the Ṛigveda, as to supply the material from which such a picture may be drawn. The writer has endeavoured to leave no strictly cosmological passage without a reference, and to add references to illustrative passages where they appeared to indicate the direction in which an explanation may be sought. In order to avoid any encumbrance of the notes by superfluous matter, references which are easily accessible in other books, such as Grassmann's Lexicon, are omitted, and those references which are intended to substantiate statements which are not likely to be the subject of doubt, are reduced to the smallest number possible. The isolation of the Ṛigveda is justified on linguistic grounds. On the other hand, the argument which is drawn from the Atharvaveda in the Introduction is based on the fact, attested by the internal character of that collection and by tradition, that the Atharvaveda lies apart from the stream of Brahmanic development: on the testimony of residents in India to the superstitious character of modern Hindoos: and on the striking similarity of the charms of the Atharvaveda to those of European nations. If, as seems most probable, the cosmological passages and hymns of the Ṛigveda are to be classified with the latest compositions in the collection, the conceptions with which the essay deals must be regarded as belonging to the latest period represented in the Ṛigveda, when the earlier hymns were still on the lips of priests whose language did not differ materially in construction from that contained in the hymns which they recited.

The writer desires here to express his sincere gratitude to those teachers who have assisted him in his general Sanskrit studies, Professors

E. B. Cowell, R. v. Roth, G. Bühler, F. Kielhorn, and K. Geldner, some of whom have also kindly suggested corrections in this essay while it was passing through the press. Above all, his thanks are due to that Trust which, in the first place, rendered it possible for him to devote himself to the study, and now has undertaken the publication of this book.

May, 1887.

TABLE OF CONTENTS.

INTRODUCTION.

CHAPTER I.

THE BUILDING OF THE WORLD.

CHAPTER II.

GENERATION.

CHAPTER III.

THE SACRIFICE.

CHAPTER IV.

THE ORDER OF THE WORLD.

APPENDIX.

THE COSMOGRAPHY OF THE ṚIGVEDA.

CORRIGENDA.

Page 25, line 23. *For* three *read* four.
Page 40, line 23. *For* XI. 81. 4. *read* IX. 81. 4.
Page 57, note 5. *For* sun *read* son.
Page 67, note 4. *For* X. 196. 4. *read* X. 169. 4.
Page 92, note 1. *For* world *read* word.

THE

COSMOLOGY OF THE ṚIGVEDA.

INTRODUCTION.

RELIGION is the behaviour of man with respect to the natural forces and influences of the world which he regards as manifestations of superhuman will. The external form of religion is characterized by rites and ceremonies which are for the most part traditions from a forgotten past; the inner life is twofold, on the one hand emotional, enthusiastic, and passionate, on the other reflective, speculative, and philosophical. The character of each of these phases is determined by the culture and civilization of the people professing the religion. The historian may approach his subject from three sides, according as he wishes to illustrate the aesthetic, moral, or mental character of the people. In the following pages the religious hymns of the Ṛigveda will be treated solely as expressions of intellectual thought. The stray guesses and vague attempts at philosophy, which are scattered here and there through the hymns of that collection, will be classified and, as far as possible, arranged in logical sequence with a view to discovering the manner of reasoning in vogue among the composers of the hymns, the nature of the inferences and proofs which they admitted. A critical investigation of the earliest recorded results of Indian thought may be expected to throw considerable light on the difficult problem of the growth of Indian philosophy, if a subject can be found which is common to the later and the earlier thinkers. Fortunately, one great problem presents itself immediately as pressing for solution in all ages, namely, the origin and formation of the existing world. The passages relating to this subject will here be brought together and arranged according to the similarity of the ideas contained in them; the most obvious links connecting analogous conceptions will be suggested; and other passages will be adduced only so far as they serve to explain allusions in the cosmological passages.

It is an essential condition of such a study that the limits of the subject should be drawn as closely as possible; that, as far as possible, every avenue should be closed upon conjecture and hypothesis; and that, whenever this is practicable, the authors of the hymns should be allowed to speak their own words. Consequently, no attempt will be made to discover the origin of the conceptions found in our book. Mythology and etymology, the investigation of the stereotyped and formal results of preceding ages of thought, find no place in such a plan. Parallels from the religious and philosophic thought of other nations, and illustrations from later books, which would have obscured the interdependence of the Vedic ideas on one another, and so rendered it more difficult for the reader to place himself in the position of the authors, are also excluded.

The almost entire neglect of the chronological sequence of the hymns in this essay, which is a more serious omission, is the unavoidable consequence of the failure that has as yet attended every attempt to find a criterion by which to determine their relative dates. It is generally supposed that the occurrence of a hymn in the tenth book affords a suspicion of the lateness of its composition. Forms and meanings of words and grammatical constructions, which are of rare occurrence in the Ṛigveda, and become more frequent later, would also seem to indicate a late date for the hymns in which they occur; but it has not yet been found possible to establish any rules of general applicability on this score. Even if we were able to determine the dates of the hymns, we should still be very far from deciding the relative ages of the ideas contained in them. The cosmological guesses strung together in the other Vedic collections, and even in the Brāhmaṇas, occasionally bear a more primitive character than those in the Ṛigveda, though the task of separating them from later accretions is encumbered with greater difficulty.

The illustrations from geology which are frequently introduced in this connection fail to apply in one important particular. The opinions held by a single man or a body of men are not lifeless as a fossil nor arranged in strata according to age; they are continually growing or dying, and shifting their relative positions through interaction one on another; they derive their vitality and force of meaning from association with the whole complex of thought in which they live. A chronological arrangement of the ideas could have no other basis than such general principles as may be abstracted from a comprehensive study of the mythology and ideology of all nations.

One question, which has given rise to much dispute, requires preliminary consideration: how far our hymns may be regarded as representative of the common thought of the people. The question admits of treatment in two ways. We may consider the statements of the Ṛishis, the composers of the hymns, about themselves and their work;[1] and we may compare their productions with the only other Veda of a sufficiently distinctive character, the Atharvaveda. If we examine the hymns of the Ṛigveda alone, we find there two clear indications of the bias of the authors in their exclusiveness and their

[1] A rich collection of passages on this subject will be found in Dr. Muir's Original Sanskṛit Texts, vol. iii., and in his article on the position of the priests in the Vedic age in the J.R.A.S. for 1866, p. 257.

glorification of the sacrifice. They represent themselves as the only mediators between man and the gods. They pride themselves on the pure orthodoxy of their religion and on the correctness of their rites. Theirs are the true or real gods, served by the true priests of a true faith, with true prayers and offerings.[1] Other worshippers and their gods are cursed as demons and worshippers of demons.[2] They are the ungodly, men who know not Indra, who deny Indra's existence, who serve no Agni, enemies of the gods, haters of the sacrifice, men of evil ways, who offer no sacrifice.[3] Upon such people the Ṛishis call down the terrible wrath of all their gods, and solemnly aver that they have never themselves been guilty of any improper worship of other gods or demons. Owing to the vagueness of the references, it is impossible to determine against whom the denunciations are levelled, whether at dissenters belonging to the same nation or tribe as the orthodox or at foreigners; they present us, however, with the picture of a violent religious contest, and serve to remind us that the Ṛishis were not the only bidders for authority among the people, even in matters of theology. If the Ṛishis had any differences among

[1] II. 26. 1. Bergaigne, La Religion védique, vol. iii. p. 184.

[2] V. 42. 10., V. 12., VII. 104. 14–16., V. 42. 10., VIII. 18. 13., II. 23. 16.

[3] *ádeva ; anindrá* cf. II. 12. 5. ; *ánagnitrā* cf. I. 147. 2. ; *devanídaḥ ; brahmadvíshaḥ ; anyávrata, avratá, ápavrata ; ayajñá.*

themselves, their common interest at any rate centred in the sacrifice. The most extravagant and offensive verses in the collection are the unrestrained praises of the liberality of kings and other rich patrons of the sacrifice, shown especially in donations of cattle to the priests. It was the endeavour of the Ṛishis to make themselves as indispensable as possible to the great ones of the earth, and for that end to magnify the sacrifice and its accompaniment, the hymn, as the only means of attaining prosperity and divine favour.[1] There are no curses so bitter as those in which they denounce the illiberal. This glorification of the sacrifice is the main burden of the whole Ṛigveda, showing itself in the assimilation of all things in heaven and earth to the sacrifice, and in the elevation of the instruments and personifications of the sacrifice to the rank of great deities. It was not in the interest of the Ṛishis to help forward the progress of speculative thought in its advance towards philosophy; but rather to hedge about their own religious conceptions with a wall of sanctity, and to bring within this compass the wandering fancies of the people, and the enquiring guesses of the thinkers. Extraneous thought and criticism was to them a source of danger; they sought, therefore, to obscure the doctrines of their theology by a multiplication of complicated allusions and dark riddles, with which

[1] Compare H. Zimmer, Altindisches Leben, pp. 168–171, 194–5.

they might occupy the minds of their hearers, at the same time gratifying the native taste for puzzle and paradox.[1] The material upon which they worked consisted in part of the myths and legends which were rooted in the traditions of the people, and partly also of the rude physics and metaphysics of the more thoughtful. These they endeavour to adapt to their own sacrificial theory.

The contents and form of the great majority of the hymns in the Ṛigveda bear distinctly the marks of a complex of doctrine in process of elaboration.[2] It would be quite conceivable that this doctrine, the work of a class of priests, was submissively accepted as alone efficacious by the mass of the people, were the Ṛigveda the only Veda extant. The Atharvaveda, however, presents us with another picture. In it we find a collection of charms and incantations for the practical uses of common life, exhibiting a spiritism and a demonolatry which the Ṛishis of the Ṛigveda scorned. We find a state of morality contrasting

[1] *parokshapriyā iva hi devāḥ pratyakshadvishaḥ*, 'For the gods love what is recondite, and hate that which is evident.'—Bṛihadār. Up. 4. 2. 2.

[2] "Neither in the language nor in the thought of the Ṛig-Veda have I been able to discover that quality of primitive natural simplicity which so many are fain to see in it. The poetry it contains appears to me, on the contrary, to be of a singularly refined character and artificially elaborated, full of allusions and reticences, of pretensions to mysticism and theosophic insight; and the manner of its expression is such as reminds one more frequently of the phraseology in use among certain small groups of initiated than the poetic language of a large community." —Barth, The Religions of India, p. xiii.

strongly with the noble moral teaching of the Ṛigveda, and a more popular treatment of the Vedic gods. We find, further, a number of speculative pieces of rank mysticism running out in wild luxuriance far beyond the sober limits of the hymns of the Ṛigveda. We are therefore justified in characterizing the hymns of the Ṛigveda as in the main the products of a special system independent of the general thought of the nation, and in carefully considering at every point how far the adjustment of thought to it may have influenced the form of expression. In this essay the word Ṛishi will, for convenience, be used particularly to denote the adherents and promoters of this system.

On the other hand, if it be granted that the hymns represent in the main a system of theology which was the work of a particular class of men, rather than the natural growth of a national consciousness, we may still find the greatest difficulty in individual cases in determining how far the system has influenced their manner of thought. The following description of the peculiar treatment of the gods in our collection may serve as an illustration of this difficulty. The deities of the Ṛigveda differ essentially from the gods of Greek or Scandinavian mythology and of the Mahābhārata in the abstract and almost impersonal nature of their characters. They are little more than factors in the physical and moral order of the world, apart from which none, except perhaps Indra, has a self-interested existence. To the Ṛishis they are pre-eminently the receivers of sacrifice; the apotheosis of the Ṛibhus is described as the attainment of the right to receive sacrifice. They have no definite forms. The mention of their clothes, or of different parts of their bodies, serves only to express the nature of their actions or characters. The strength of Indra is illustrated by the shaking of his blonde mustachios; his insatiable thirst for soma causes the poet to glorify the enormous capacity of his belly. Savitar raises his arms, the beams of the sun, to give life to the world. Rudra and the Maruts are clad in bright armour and carry spears, and crack their shining whips of light over their horses to represent the lightning. The Dawn lets fall her clothes to display her beauty. Mitra and Varuṇa are throned in heaven; the other gods, so far as they are not identified with individual objects, wander through the world at will. We hear nothing of temples of the gods, and it is almost certain that the hymns recognize no idols; the gods were themselves present in the different phenomena of the world.

The peculiarly impersonal nature of the gods is seen in the deification of purely abstract notions and agencies. The most striking examples of such gods are those whose names are formed with the suffix *tar*; the divine agents of the processes designated by the verbal roots from which their names are derived. The most prominent of these are Savitar, 'the quickener,' and Tvashṭar, 'the carpenter.' That both gods were considered as such agents appears from the frequent play on the connection between their names and the related verbal forms; and from the constant addition to their names of the substantive *devá*, in passages where we may with equal plausibility translate 'the carpenter god,' 'the quickening god,' or 'god Savitar,' 'god Tvashṭar.' Tvashṭar is the god who produces the various objects in nature which show the skill of an artificer; Savitar is, however, with few exceptions,[1] always identified with the great quickener of the world, the sun; and thus the abstract character of his conception is somewhat obscured. The frequent ascription of the action of ordaining (*dhā*) the things in the world to different gods led to the conception of a separate god, the Ordainer or Establisher, Dhātar. Vidhātar is in like manner the Disposer. We find a *devá* Netar three times invoked in one hymn,[2] apparently as the Guide of the course of life; and a *devá* Trātar, to whom prayers are addressed for protection against foes.[3] Other examples of deities invoked by the Ṛishis, whose names bear a similarly abstract character, are Brahmaṇaspati or Bṛihaspati, 'the lord of the sacrificial prayer,' Prajāpati 'the lord of things born,' Anumati 'graciousness,' Aramati 'prayer,' Īḷā 'adoration,' Çraddhā 'faith,' and Vāc 'voice.'

1 *e.g.* IV. 54., III. 33. 6.
2 V. 50.
3 IV. 55. 5, 7., I. 106. 7., VIII. 18. 20.

The abstract nature of the Vedic gods in general shows itself in the indefiniteness of the sphere of activity of each one, in the poverty of their individual attributes, and in the readiness with which these attributes are transferred from one god to another. This is the explanation of the principle familiar from Professor Max Müller's writings under the name of 'henotheism,' by which the god invoked on a particular occasion is represented as exercising the functions of other gods, and assuming their attributes. The more impersonal and abstract the conception of the god, the easier it is to attribute his entire activity to another. This is particularly striking in the case of one ancient god, Bhaga, who has become in the Ṛigveda little more than a source from which descriptions of the functions of other gods are obtained, or a standard of comparison by which their greatness is enhanced. His name has survived in the Slavonic languages as a general name for god, a sense which it also has in the Avesta. To judge from the Ṛigveda, Bhaga would seem to be a survival from an ancient sun-worship, of which we shall find traces in the course of the essay. His name is frequently mentioned with that of Savitar, apparently as an epithet to express Savitar's bountiful gift of sunshine to men. He is invoked along with Pūshan and the Ādityas, Mitra, Varuṇa, and Aryaman. The dawn is his sister.[1] The eye of heaven is adorned with Bhaga's

[1] I. 123. 5.; cf. VII. 41. 2.

light. The hymns mount up to Vishṇu as on Bhaga's road.[1] Most frequently, however, comparison with Bhaga is intended to express a vague glorification of the bounty of Indra and Agni; the only special points of comparison are that Indra carries the two worlds, heaven and earth, as Bhaga; and that Agni is the leader of the tribes of heaven, as Bhaga.[2]

This apparent confusion of the functions of the gods shows itself in three ways. In the first place, there are common divine actions or attributes which may with equal propriety be ascribed to two or more gods invoked separately or together, to all the members of different classes of gods, such as the sacrificial gods, and the warrior-gods, or to all the gods as gods. In such cases there is no real confusion. Secondly, there are attributes and actions expressed in similar phrases, which, however, belong to different gods through the development of their characters from different original conceptions in such a way as to cover common ground. Of this nature are the approximation of Tvashṭar and Savitar, and the application of the name 'father' to different gods. This tendency was assisted by the occasional existence in the mind of a poet of a traditional verse or expression applied originally to another god, but expressing more or less exactly the thought the poet

[1] I. 136. 2.; III. 54. 14.; cf. X. 151. 1.
[2] I. 62. 7.; III. 20. 4.

wished to utter. The confusion is in this case real, but it is not the result of a direct transference of functions. Lastly, there is the conscious application to one god of the attributes of another, often of the most characteristic attributes of the other god, either with the addition of the name of the other god, or with some appellative or expression familiar to the Ṛishis in association with him. The god invoked, who in such cases is usually Agni, Soma, or Indra, unites with his own functions those of another god or gods. Agni, Soma, and Bṛihaspati are expressly identified with other gods as including their entire activity, even without the insertion of any adverb of comparison, as also it is said of Savitar that he "becomes Mitra, becomes Pūshan."[1] The transference here is occasional and of a rhetorical character, and is thus entirely distinct from the syncretism of the later divine Triad.

This fusion is, however, but one phase of a movement of thought to be traced through the whole collection, a harmonizing movement by which it is endeavoured to concentrate the theological ideas recognized by the Ṛishis. It is the result of two tendencies, both of which would seem to mark our hymns as belonging rather to the end of an epoch in the thought of the nation than to a period of

[1] II. 1., V. 3. 1, 2., I. 163. 3.; IX. passim; X. 98. 1.; *mitró bhavasi pūshā́ bhavasi* V. 81. 4, 5.

active production.[1] The one tendency which is peculiarly characteristic of India is the economical desire to collect and preserve the entire theological stock of the nation that nothing be lost, rather than to strike out a new path in disregard of previous results. Legends and mythical conceptions, as well as deities, derived originally from different orders of thought, are placed side by side, approximated to one another and confused together. The other tendency is the endeavour to define the unity of nature, which to the layman was apparently typified in the light, but which the Ṛishi endeavoured to associate with the sacrifice. The various products of this latter tendency are particularly characteristic of the difference between the cosmologies and cosmological formulae of the Ṛigveda and those of the Atharvaveda. In the Ṛigveda, as we have seen, the divine actions are transferable from one god to another; in the mystical hymns of the Atharvaveda the several elements of the world are identified with a few abstractions, Skambha 'the support,' Prāṇa 'the breath of life,' Kāla 'time,' Ucchishṭa 'the remains of the sacrifice,'

[1] "For the great majority of the hymns of the Ṛigveda it becomes, in my opinion, more and more evident, that they mark not the rise, nor the zenith, but rather the decline of the oldest Indian lyrical art. This appears from the unvaried uniformity and monotony of thought and metaphor, the absence of originality in most of the hymns of the Ṛigveda; and these rather negative qualities are not indeed limited to particular books, they extend, so far as I can see, in greater or less degree, over the whole collection."—Bradke's Dyaus Asura, p. 2.

and others, each of which is for the time tentatively regarded as the substratum of the universe, its cause and end. Neither of these phases can be accurately described as pantheistic. In the earlier book the gods are not categorically (with one or two exceptions, *e.g.* Aditi I. 89. 10.) identified with the universe; in the later the abstractions and strange figures with which the elements of nature are identified cannot be described as gods. The logical development of the one phase of thought ends in monotheism, of the other in atheism.

CHAPTER I.

THE BUILDING OF THE WORLD.

THE philosophy of nature may be described as the classification of natural forces and agencies. The classifications of science are based upon identity or uniformity of principle discovered by analysis and inductive reasoning; unscientific classifications or mental associations are the results of superficial comparison. The former we commonly call explanations, the latter resemblances, analogies, or metaphors. In an age destitute of science this distinction vanishes; the metaphor partakes of the nature of an explanation. The importance of the metaphors employed in the Ṛig-veda is seen in the constancy of their application as compared with the ornamental or descriptive metaphors of modern poetry; fixed comparisons are consecrated to particular uses and endued with a sanction which can only be explained as the result of a very special sense of their propriety. Thus in describing the formation of the world we find the Vedic poets recurring perpetually to the metaphor of building in all its details, showing that they accepted this comparison as the form of expression most applicable to creation. If we remember that the Vedic house was made of wood, it is not difficult to picture to ourselves in outline the different stages in the process of its erection: first, the felling of the trees for wood, and the measuring of the site; next, the fixing of the main-posts in the four corners supported by leaning buttresses, and of the two door-posts in the front; and lastly, the covering-in of the whole with cross-beams, rafters, laths, and some kind of mud or thatch to fill up the crevices. We shall see all these stages recur in the allusions to the formation of the world.

That the world should have been created from nothing is an idea which finds no place in the Ṛigveda; the Ṛishis are, however, at a loss to explain whence the divine builders obtained the imperishable material for their work. "What indeed was the wood? What too was that tree from which they fashioned the heaven and the earth? They two stand fast and grow not old for ever, while many days and mornings wax old."[1] The measuring of

[1] X. 31. 7.; cf. X. 81. 4. Whether the word *vána* in the Ṛigveda is ever to be translated 'forest' is doubtful. The use of the word for cloud would seem to be due to the following associations. The rain is pictured as contained in wooden vats. The lightning burns in the clouds as fire in wood. The clouds are blown by the wind as the branches and foliage of trees. The difficult verse X. 28. 8. appears to refer to the clearing up of the sky through the thunderstorm: "The gods came carrying axes, splitting the clouds (*vánā*); they came with their attendants; they set good wood in heaven, where there was refuse (perhaps 'underwood' Pet. Lex.) they burnt it up." The myth of the world-tree is apparently alluded to in X. 135. 1., I. 24. 7., and I. 164. 20; cf. A. V. X. 7. 38.

'the two ancient dwelling-places,' heaven and earth, in the different senses of the word, is a frequent topic in the hymns. Thus we read of Indra, as the representative of the gods, "he it is who measured the six broad spaces, from which no existing thing is excluded; he it is who made the wide expanse of earth and the lofty dome of the sky, even he;"[1] and again, with confusion of the measure and the thing measured, "two measures are thine, O Indra, broad and well-measured, the heaven by thy greatness and the earth by thy skill."[2] The measuring instrument is represented by the sun traversing the earth in his course, and shooting his straight beams from East to West. "Varuṇa, standing in the region of the air, measureth out the earth with the sun as with a measuring-rod."[3] Hence the measurers of the world *par excellence* are the sun-gods, as Vishṇu, who "measured the regions of the earth, and made fast the dwelling-place on high, stepping forth, the mighty strider, in three steps." The natural place to begin the surveying is in the front of the house; and so the gods began their measurement of the earth from the East. "Indra measured out (*vimimāya*) as it were a house with measures from the front."[4] The idea

[1] VI. 47. 3, 4. For the explanation of the 'six spaces' and other cosmographical references, see Appendix.

[2] X. 29. 6.

[3] V. 85. 5.

[4] *prā́cah̤* II. 15. 3., cf. VII. 99. 2. *prā́cīm kakúbham pṛithivyā́ḥ.*

of measuring is closely allied to that of spreading out the earth, revealing it to the eyes of man, a function also ascribed to the gods connected with the sun and the lightning, in particular to Indra, Agni, and the Maruts. The site seems to have been consecrated by being anointed with ghee,[1] which in our hymns represents the rain or light given by the gods. The fathers (Manes; see Ch. III.) "anointed heaven and earth to rule over them; they measured them with measuring-rods; they made them fast and broad; they set the great worlds apart, firmly fixed for security."[2] Connected with the action of measuring is that of setting in the corner-posts, frequently expressed by a different form (*mi*) of the same root. The doors of the cosmic house are the portals of the East through which the morning light enters into the world. "The Dawn shone with brilliance, and opened for us the doors."[3] The doors "open high and wide with their frames."[4] They are broad as the earth, "extending wide and above all, many in number, yea very many; through the doors flow the streams of ghee."[5] They are particularly glorified in the Āprī-hymns, as the gates through which the gods approach, the arrangement of the place of sacri-

[1] A. V. III. 12. 1.
[2] III. 38. 3., cf. I. 190. 2.
[3] I. 113. 4., IV. 51. 2., V. 45. 1.
[4] *ắtaiḥ* IX. 5. 5.
[5] I. 188. 5.

fice being assimilated to the measurement of the world. Lastly, the covering-in of the house with cross-beams and a thatching of bamboo-canes is alluded to negatively in the designation of the sky as the beamless or the rafterless. "He was a clever workman in the world who produced this heaven and earth, and fixed the two regions of air in the beamless space."[1] The air is said to be woven in the trees or clouds. "Thou, O Indra, didst fasten firmly the region of air in the frame of heaven and earth."[2]

The criterion of excellence in the human house was the firmness and compactness of its structure. So we are continually told of one god and another how he holds the heaven and the earth fast; and the security of the never-falling sky is a perpetual source of wonder to the human builders. "Indra spread out the broad earth, a great marvel, and supported the sky, erect and mighty." "He supported the heaven and the earth apart." "That which thou makest secure is secure."[3] The heaven is itself called *vidharman*, or simply *dhárman*, 'the support' or 'the firmament.'[4] But the compactness of the building was useless unless the foundations were sure. "Savitar

[1] *avaṁçá* IV. 56. 3., II. 15. 2.; *askambhaná* X. 149. 1.; cf. Chānd. Up. 3. 1. 1.

[2] V. 85. 2.; I. 56. 5.

[3] VI. 17. 7.; V. 29. 4.; VIII. 45. 6.

[4] This sense seems necessary for *dhárman* in VIII. 6. 20. The fuller expression *dhárman divó dharúṇe* (X. 170. 2., V. 15. 2.), 'the sure firmament of the sky' or 'the support supporting the sky,' is abbreviated into

made the earth fast with bands." "Vishṇu fixed it on all sides with pegs." "Bṛihaspati supports firmly in their places the ends of the earth."[1] When all was finished, the world was furnished with gifts of light, rain, and air.[2]

Such is a brief outline of the metaphor of the house as it pictured itself to the lively fancy of the poets. A more special characteristic of the mode of thought in the Ṛigveda is the invariable introduction into all cosmological conceptions of the fires of heaven and earth, the sun, the lightning or the thunderbolt, and the fire of sacrifice. The solar and meteorological explanations of mythology have been the subject of so much controversy of late that it is necessary to call the reader's attention once for all to the fact that the frequent references in this essay to the sun and the lightning, as the natural phenomena uppermost in the minds of the Ṛishis, are in no sense solar or fulgural explanations of mythology, or of the origins of the gods; they merely draw attention to the conceptions associated with different gods (perhaps conventionally) in the Ṛigveda. The first act of the Indian on entering his new house was the introduction of the sacred fire, Agni, "who was ever

dhármaṇi in III. 38. 2., and perhaps in I. 159. 3., cf. IX. 97. 22. For *vídharman* see Grassmann's Lexicon; Bergaigne contests this meaning for *vídharman* also, La Religion vệdique, III. 218. n. 2.

[1] *yantraiḥ* X. 149. 1.; *mayúkhaiḥ* VII. 99. 3.; IV. 50. 1; cf. X. 89. 1.

[2] I. 56. 5., III. 30. 11., II. 15. 2. etc.

to be worshipped in the house," "the master of the house."[1] The first act of the gods after the formation of the world was to produce the celestial Agni, the sun or the lightning. From the hearth in the middle of the house the flames and smoke streamed up towards the roof, presenting the picture of a pillar supporting the ceiling. Agni is "the head of heaven and the navel of the earth;"[2] he, as his liquid counterpart, Soma, is 'the bearer of heaven' and the support of the world. "He was set down among men as a wise priest, welcome in the sacrifice for his knowledge; he shot up his straight light like Savitar, and supported his smoke toward heaven like a builder."[3] The sun is the gold or bronzen pillar of Mitra and Varuṇa's throne; the sky itself is compared to a firmly set pillar.[4] This function of Agni was symbolized by the erection of a post in the place of sacrifice, the *vánaspáti* of the Āprī-hymns, which was anointed with ghee to represent his light.

The action of building the cosmic house, corresponding to the rough work of the Indian peasant, is attributed for the most part to the gods in general, to Indra as the representative of the gods,

[1] *gṛihápati, vástosh pátiḥ.* VII. 1. 2. cf. III. 1. 17.

[2] I. 59. 2.

[3] IV. 6. 2. cf. IV. 13. 5., VI. 47. 5., X. 88. 1., III. 5. 10.

[4] V. 62. 7, 8.; V. 45. 2.

or to Mitra and Varuṇa, as the ordainers of all that is in the world. But there are other gods, whose special character is based on their skill in the finer works of the joiner's art, such as would be delegated by the peasant to the professional workman. These are Tvashṭar and the Ṛibhus. Tvashṭar is the clever-handed carpenter-god, who, in particular, manufactured with his hatchet the thunderbolt of Indra, but also, in general, "adorned heaven and earth, the parents, and all things with their forms,"[1] whence heaven and earth are called 'the artificer's pair.' In the sacrifice he created the hymn of praise, which is technically described as a piece of joinery. "Tvashṭar produced thee (Bṛihaspati) from all existing things, from hymn after hymn, the skilled artificer.[2] He is also one of the gods who generated the sacred fire.[3] But his chief contribution to the sacrifice is the soma, Tvashṭar's mead.[4] His special function in the natural world is the formation of the embryo in the womb, whence he is regarded as the giver of children and of increase in cattle.[5] This function and its connection with the soma will call for further treatment in the next chapter. The menial character

[1] X. 110. 9., IV. 42, 3., III. 55. 19.; cf. V. 42. 13.
[2] II. 23. 17.
[3] X. 2. 7., 46. 9., I. 95. 2.
[4] I. 117. 22., cf. X. 53. 9.
[5] I. 188. 9.

of Tvashṭar's activity, and his association with the harem of the gods, covered him with a certain ridicule in the eyes of the Ṛishis. There is no hymn devoted to his praise in the whole collection. Indra is represented as surpassing him in his own special department, the making of the soma or the rain in the clouds: "I placed the bright milk in these cows, which even god Tvashṭar could not place in them." While a baby Indra stole the soma out of the bowls in Tvashṭar's house, where Tvashṭar had tried to hide it.[1]

The same view of the menial office of the divine workmen is seen in the ascription to the Ṛibhus of a human birth, and in the conception that they obtained their immortality by their service of the gods. The praises of the Ṛibhus consist in enumerations of a certain number of actions, expressed in fixed mythological figures, the discussion of which lies outside the scope of this essay. They make hymns and soma like Tvashṭar; they produce the wonderful chariot of the Açvins, and Indra's thunderbolt and horses. They are even said in one place to have fashioned the Açvins themselves,[2] and they shape the cow of plenty in the sky. It is said of a strong king given to the people by the Maruts, as also of the streams, that he was formed by Vibhvan, one

[1] X. 49. 10.; III. 48. 4., IV. 18. 3., I. 84. 15.

[2] IV. 34. 9., cf. VI. 3. 8.

of their number.[1] In particular, their renovating of their aged and decrepid parents, and of the old cow, which they reunited to her calf, would seem to refer to the new birth of the world through the recurrence of the seasons; and they are once said to have made heaven and earth.[2] We have the names of three Ṛibhus; but the varied character of their workings in the different departments of nature is emphasized by the mystic number, thrice seven, of their gifts, and we find the expression 'all the Ṛibhus' employed as if of an indefinite number. Their names are severally used in the plural; and one passage has the remarkable expression, 'Ṛibhu with the Ṛibhus, Vibhva with the Vibhus, the powers with power,'[3] which can leave little doubt that the number of these 'men of the air' was in one form of their legends as vague as that of the wonderful works of nature. Indra figures as their chief, or, in the phrase of the Ṛigveda, they are his sons; he as a Ṛibhu bestows gifts on man and beast.[4]

Two legends concerning the Ṛibhus deserve special mention: their contest with Tvashṭar, when they made three cups for the soma from his one, and their production of grass on the meadows by refreshing the

[1] *vibhvatashṭá* V. 58. 4., 42. 12.

[2] IV. 34. 9.

[3] *ṛibhúr ṛibhúbhiḥ . . . . víbhvo vibhúbhiḥ çávasā çávāṁsi.* VII. 48. 2.

[4] IV. 37. 4., I. 121. 2.

earth with streams after twelve days' rest, as guests, in the house of Agohya. In the first case we may discover the explanation of Tvashṭar's defeat in the superior number of the Ṛibhus, representing the conquest of a combination of inferior beings over a single-handed mighty power. The legend is usually explained as referring to the three worlds; it may possibly refer merely to a change of ritual.[1] The Ṛibhus, as we shall see was the case with Tvashṭar, are brought into special connection with the sun, the main agent of productiveness in nature. They are 'bright as the sun' (*sū́racakshasaḥ*), the sons of Sudhanvan, the 'good archer'; "with their father's energy (*taraṇitrā́*) they obtained his wealth and mounted up into the region of heaven;" it is, in particular, Savitar who befriends them and procures them immortality; and we read of "the dispositions of the Ṛibhus according to the succession of the dawns."[2]

We are thus brought to the end of the first explanation of the formation of the world. The reader cannot fail to have been struck with the disinterested, objective character of the description; the end of creation is not man; the Ṛishis do not question the motive of the gods in forming the world. Divine

1 F. Nève, Essai sur le mythe des Ribhavas, Paris, 1847.

2 I. 110. 6., cf. IV. 33. 1.; I. 110. 2, 3., cf. Ait. Br. 3. 3. 30.; *vidhā́nā ṛibhūṇā́m* IV. 51. 6.

actions are magnified copies of human actions; as, therefore, a man must build his house, so the gods have built the universal house. The similarity, we may almost say the identity, of the divine and human occupations, with this difference that the gods lack the object for which men pursue their work, will be also illustrated by the next chapter on generation as a cosmological principle.

CHAPTER II.

GENERATION.

In the preceding chapter attention was drawn to the familiar logical distinction between induction and analogy or metaphor. It was shown by an illustration how the metaphor, which in modern literature is employed as a figure of language, was in the Ṛigveda of great importance as a mode of thought. The present chapter will afford an illustration of analogical reasoning. Analogy is the comparison of effects or of classes of effects, which we are unable to analyse, but which appear so similar as to lead to the presumption that they are due to similar causes. In formal expression this method of reasoning usually makes use of a type, or particularly well-known and obvious example of the class in which cause and effect are found to coexist; one striking instance is singled out as representative of the process which seems to relate the cause to the effect. In the argument which forms the subject of this chapter the process which is described is that of generation; the type is the union of light and water at dawn and in the thunderstorm;

the effect which requires explanation is the origin of the world.

We have further seen in the description of Agni as the pillar which supports the heavens the importance of visible pictorial presentment in cosmological speculation. It is the visible periodical union of the two most antagonistic elements of nature, fire and water, seen in the glistening dew of the dawn, the brightness of the morning mist, and the flash of lightning piercing the rain-cloud, which explains the complicated sensuous symbolism of those hymns in which the generation of the world is described. We shall find that light or warmth and moisture, the chief factors of generation in the cosmology of the Ṛigveda as in the systems of the Ionic philosophers, are not here, as they are there, the primary elements out of which the world formed itself, but are always bound up with the phenomena of the sky, the sun in the clouds, and the lightning in the rain. In illustration of this the chapter before us will treat first of the birth of the sun as the type of all subsequent births, next of the action of fire or light and water as productive agencies, and lastly of the general principle of generation as applied to explain the origin of the world.

There are three principal applications of the metaphor of parentage in the Ṛigveda, temporal, generic, and local. In the temporal sense it expresses the appearance of one phenomenon before another; the dawn is the mother of the sun and of the morning sacrifice, the night is the mother of the morning,[1] and the like. The parent may correspond to an efficient cause, as when the Maruts, the gods of the storm-cloud, are said to give birth to darkness, or again to the material cause, expressing the transformation of one object into another, as when the rain is said to be born of the cloud.[2]

Again, the father is head and representative of the sons of the family, as the mother of the daughters; his personality is continued in them.[3] Thus the metaphor obtains a generic sense, expressing the most prominent member of a group; Vāyu is the father of the winds, or of the storm-gods, Rudra is the father of the Maruts and Rudras, soma of the plants and of the prayers; Sarasvatī is the mother of the rivers. The sons may be considered as inheriting the qualities of the father, as when Tvashṭar's epithet *viçvárūpa* is separated from him and becomes the name of his son;[4] or again, as in the Semitic languages, the place of the father may be occupied by an abstract quality, as when Agni, the Maruts and others are

[1] VII. 78. 3.; I. 123. 9.

[2] VII. 94. 1.

[3] II. 33. 1.

[4] *yad etaj jāyate 'patyaṁ sa evāyam iti çrutiḥ,* "according to the Veda the offspring which is born to a man is the man himself."—Mahābhārata, Çāntip. 10862; cf. Bṛihadār. Up. 2. 1. 7.

called 'the sons of strength,' or Pūshan who sets men 'in a large place' is called 'the child of setting free,' and Indra the child of cow-getting.[1]

Lastly, the metaphor has a local sense. The quiver is called the father of the arrows,[2] carrying them as a father carries his child in his arms. The earth is the mother of the trees and of all things that she bears on her broad bosom, and the heaven the father of all things that move in the sky, the sun, the Maruts, morning and evening.[3]

But heaven and earth do not merely contain all things, they also supply the nourishment by which they grow; the harvest-time, for instance, can be called the child of the earth.[4] The transition is easy from the local application of the metaphor to the temporal. Heaven and earth are the dwelling-places in which all births take place, they are also the first-born in the beginning, of equal age and common origin; or, what amounts to the same thing, the question is mooted, which of the two could have been the older;[5] or again, by a characteristic confusion

[1] *vimuco napāt* I. 42. 1., VI. 55. 1.; *goshaṇo napāt* IV. 32. 22. We may perhaps trace the incipient misconception of this idiom, which does not belong to the later language, in the explanation of the phrase *sáhasas putráḥ* as applied to Agni from the force exercised in rubbing the fire-sticks (V. 11. 6.). We must not, however, interpret the etymological fancies of the Ṛishis too seriously.

[2] VI. 75. 5.

[3] I. 185. 2.

[4] I. 173. 3.

[5] I. 185. 1.

of thought, they are represented as the two fruitful parents, who produced the world for their offspring.[1] The difficulty at once arose of fixing the relation of heaven and earth as the universal parents to the gods, who, from another point of view, have also a claim to be considered the fathers of the world. The Ṛishis contented themselves with a favourite paradox: the children begat their parents. "Indra begat his father and his mother from his own body."[2]

The first-born of heaven and earth is the sun. This birth is one of the most frequent topics of the Ṛigveda, hinted at for the most part rather than described in a series of complicated riddles playing perpetually on the identification of the three kinds of Agni, in the sun, the lightning, and the fire or soma of the sacrifice; on the comparison of heaven and earth to the two rubbing-sticks that produced the fire, or to the two stones between which the soma was pressed; and other recondite parallelisms enriching the formal expression more than the meaning of the hymns. A great source of perplexity in the interpretation is the confusion of the dawns or night and morning, which give birth to the sun,[3] with the waters, the mists of the sky or the rain-clouds which carry the embryo of the lightning.

[1] I. 159. 2.
[2] I. 159. 3., X. 54. 3.
[3] V. 1. 4.

They are both alike represented as the cows of Agni, his mothers, his nurses, sisters, or wenches. The light itself is considered as a liquid, as in the familiar English expressions a 'stream' or 'flood of light,' 'pouring light.' "The sun mounts upon a liquid flood."[1]

The centre-point of the theory of cosmological generation, as has been said, is the combination of the light with the waters, which presented itself to the eyes of the poets in the birth of the lightning from the rain-cloud, and in the exhalations which surround the light of the sun. Agni has his home in the waters; he is 'the child of the waters,' 'the one eye of heaven, who grows by the action of the streams.'[2] The reference to the lightning is sufficiently obvious; the part played by the sun in the paradox, apart from such general expressions as 'the waters about the sun' contrasted with the waters below on earth, is described as the shooting or weaving of his rays through the waters of heaven.[3] The allusion to the dew is established by the close connection of the dawn with the waters, in which she is represented as bathing.[4] The marriage of the sky with the earth, the father and mother of the sun, presented itself in two ways. First, the sky

[1] VII. 60. 4. = V. 45. 10.
[2] IX. 9. 4., where Soma represents the sun; I. 23. 17.
[3] III. 22. 3., X. 27. 21.; VII. 47, 4., IV. 38. 10., X. 178. 3.
[4] VI. 64. 4., I. 124. 5., 48. 3; V. 80. 5.

embraces the earth on all sides, and both are united in the twilight of the East before the dawn. Secondly, the fall of the rain and the shedding of light in the form of sunshine or lightning are the visible causes of the fertilization of the soil. The sun draws the dew as milk from his mother earth, and obtains his light, which as we have seen is also regarded as a liquid, from his father the sky.[1] These two, the light and the dew or rain, are interchangeably represented as milk or semen, celestial ambrosia, ghee,[2] or soma-juice.

The conception of the rising sun in the morning dew is personified in the figure of Gandharva, a discussion of whose character will be the best illustration of the birth of the sun as the type of generation. In the only entire hymn which is addressed to him, he receives the name of Vena, which occurs again in I. 83. 5. as an epithet of the rising sun. In other passages it is translated by the St. Petersburg Lexicon 'longing, desire (or desirous), wish.' It is used as an epithet of the dawns, of Soma, and of Bṛihaspati, and seems to be applied also to the songs or the singers. The hymn describes in a succession of poetical images his rise from the morning mist up to the sky, where his light is merged in the all-embracing brilliance of the heavens.

[1] I. 160. 3., IV. 3. 10., X. 11. 1.

[2] IV. 58.

X. 123. 1. "Vena, born in light, hath driven hither the calves of the speckled cow in the chariot of the air;[1] at the meeting of the sun with the waters, the singers caress (*lit.* 'lick') him here as a child with hymns.

2. Vena stirreth a ripple from out the (aerial) sea;[2] the child of the clouds hath appeared along the ridge of the bright sky;[3] on high, on the summit of nature's course, he shone; and the hosts sang to the bosom of their common father (the sky).

3. The many mothers of the calf, who have one home,[4] were there, exulting in their common child; rising to the summit of nature's course the songs sip (*lit.* lick) the sweet ambrosia.

4. The singers knowing his form yearned for him; they have found the roar of the wild buffalo (Soma); performing the sacrifice they are come to the stream. Gandharva hath found the forms of ambrosia.

5. Apsaras, the maiden, smiling on her paramour, beareth him in high heaven; he is come as a loved one to the bosom of his loved one;[5] he settleth there upon his golden wing, even Vena.

6. As with longing in their hearts (*vénantaḥ*) they gaze on thee, as a bird flying up to heaven, the gold-

[1] cf. II. 40. 3. The force of *ayám* is 'Behold here.'

[2] cf. IV. 58. 1, 11.

[3] cf. VIII. 100. 5.

[4] The dawns cf. VII. 2. 5., or, as Ludwig suggests, the waters. The two are, as has been said, practically indistinguishable.

[5] *i.e.* his father, the sky; cf. V. 47. 3., III. 1. 9., VIII. 69. 7.

winged messenger of Varuṇa, to Yama's home, a soaring eagle;

7. Upright hath Gandharva mounted into the sky pointing his glancing weapons; clad in a sweet-smelling mantle, beautiful to look upon, he produceth fair forms as the light.[1]

8. When as a drop[2] he cometh to the aerial ocean, gazing with a vulture's eye in heaven, his light rejoicing in its gleaming brilliance worketh brightness in the highest region."[3]

Similar references to Gandharva as the rising sun occur in I. 163. 2., where he holds the bridle of the horse of the sun; and in X. 177. 2., where he sings the morning song of the sun-bird; "the bird beareth a song in his heart, Gandharva sang it while yet in the womb;" "Gandharva mounts up to the sky, he beholds all the forms of Soma, his light shines abroad with gleaming brilliance, he illu-

[1] *surabhí* appears to be a play on the word *gandhá*, occurring in the name Gandharva. The third pāda is applied to Indra in VI. 29. 3., including the comparison with *svàr*. That this comparison is no hindrance to the identification of Gandharva with the sun is proved by I. 50. 5., where it is applied to *sū́rya*.

[2] Ludwig and Grassmann translate *drapsá* 'spark': "drops of fire are sparks."—Pet. Lex. s.v. Cf. Çat. Br. IV. 1. 1. 25.

[3] Literally, "worketh fairness in itself;" cf. *aruṇā́ni kṛṇvan* of Vāta X. 168. 1. The interpretation given above is the one which appears to me to agree best with the different images occurring in the hymn, and with the other references to Gandharva, and is confirmed by A. V. II. 1., IV. 1.; Grassmann in his translation, vol. ii. p. 400, inclines to connect Gandharva with the rainbow. The difference between the two interpretations scarcely affects the argument of the following pages.

minates heaven and earth, the parents, brilliantly."[1] The Gandharvas receive the epithet *vāyúkeça*, 'whose hair is as the wind,' or 'is borne upon the wind' (III. 38. 6., see next chapter); and in X. 139. 4–6. Gandharva Viçvāvasu is addressed as "the heavenly Gandharva, measuring the realm of the air."

Our hymn illustrates the two senses in which the sun is brought into connection with the waters; first, as penetrating with his beams the watery masses of the sky, and secondly, in the assimilation of his light to the waters, as soma or ambrosia, whence the depths of light become the aerial ocean. This association is stereotyped in the union of the Gandharvas and the Apsarases, a type of marriage, and in the later mythology of sexual enjoyment. An Apsaras, *ápyā yóshā*,[2] 'the water-nymph,' is mentioned in X. 10. 4. as having given birth with Gandharva to Yama, the progenitor of the human race, in the waters; and Vasishṭha, in a late hymn, VII. 33. verse 12, is represented as born from an Apsaras. Through his connection with the light and the waters Gandharva finds his parallel in the soma, which symbolizes at the same time the fructifying waters of heaven and liquid light. The identification of the two is most striking in IX. 85. 9–12, a hymn addressed to Soma, where the

[1] IX. 85. 12.
[2] X. 11. 2. is obscure.

expressions used of Gandharva Vena in X. 123. are with small modifications transferred to Soma. In IX. 86. 36. Soma is called "the heavenly Gandharva of the waters, whose eye is over men (*nṛicákshasam*, but see note 6 on page 68), born to rule over all created things:" "the daughter of the sun brought the soma, Gandharva received it." "Gandharva it is who protecteth the place of Soma, who guardeth the birthplaces of the gods, where he is invisible." "The wise (singers) sip with their songs the rich milk of heaven and earth on the sure place of the Gandharva."[1] On the other hand, in VIII. 1. 11. and 66. 5. he figures as the gaoler of the soma, and is smitten like Tvashṭar by Indra, who sets the sun free. In IX. 78. 3. the Apsarases appear in the same relation to Soma as to Gandharva.[2]

We can now understand the significance of Gandharva in the marriage ceremony. The light of the sun is considered as a main fructifying influence, not only in the trees and plants, but also in the human womb, as when it is said of Vishṇu, that he brings the parents together for rich fruitfulness, that he protects the embryo in the womb, and forms the female breast; of Pūshan, that he grants brides to his worshippers and has given birth to all things; and of the Açvins, that they have placed the embryo in

[1] IX. 113. 3.; IX. 83. 4.; I. 22. 14.; cf. X. 80. 6.; IV. 58. 4., V. S. XII. 98.

[2] cf. X. 30. 5.

all things.[1] The waters alone, especially as personified in Parjanya, the god of the rain-cloud, will be shown later to bear the same character. Gandharva represents the union of these two influences. We pass on to the other forms in which this union of the light or the sun with the waters or the dawn is expressed. In verses 40 and 41 of the classical marriage hymn, or rather collection of marriage formulae, X. 85, Sūryā, the typical bride, the daughter of the sun, the dawn who rides in the chariot of the Açvins, is given in marriage first to Soma,[2] then to Gandharva, next to Agni, and lastly to the child of man. In VI. 58. 3, 4, it is another sun-god, Pūshan, to whom the gods gave Sūryā as a bride.[3] Soma and Pūshan are associated together in II. 40 as two cosmogonic powers giving birth to the world. Again, as we have seen Gandharva called the father of Yama, so Vivasvat, a name of the sun or of the lightning, is frequently mentioned as his father; thus

[1] I. 155. 3.; VII. 36. 9., X. 184. 1., IX. 67. 10-12; I. 157. 5.

[2] Compare verse 9. "Soma was the bridegroom, the Açvins the two interceders, when Savitar gave the willing bride Sūryā to her lord." Soma is usually explained in this hymn in its later application as a name of the moon. The different formulae here collected into one hymn cannot be considered as all dating from the same period. The association of Soma with the sun-gods points to the conclusion that he has here the same significance as in other hymns of the Ṛigveda, though many verses of this hymn and their compilation may be of later date. There is a doubt in verses 21 and 22 whether we should explain Gandharva Viçvāvasu as the protector of virgins, or, as in the later literature, the violator of virgins.

[3] cf. X. 85. 26, 27., VI. 55. 4.

the union of Sūryā with Gandharva finds its parallel in the union of Tvashṭar's daughter Saraṇyū (acc. to Sonne, the storm-cloud; acc. to Prof. Müller, the dawn) with Vivasvat, the fruit of which is Yama.[1] The nature of Tvashṭar's character was, as we have seen, so indefinite that he might have been introduced as an agent in any natural phenomena, which were regarded as products of artistic skill. His special function was the formation of the embryo in the womb, and it is in this connection that we observe his approximation to the lightning and still more to the sun. We have seen that he is the handiworkman who made Indra's thunderbolt and the soma. He is very frequently associated with the goddesses of heaven, the Gnās, among whom we find mention in verse VII. 34. 22., of Rodasī and Varuṇānī the female counterparts of Rudra and Varuṇa, and also of Aramati, the goddess of prayer.[2] He is invoked to make the marriage union fruitful and to grant increase of cattle. He is the father.[3] His approximation to the sun is seen in the combination of his name with Savitar's. The two are invoked together in XI. 81. 4. Under the triple name Tvashṭar Savitar Viçvarūpa, where the epithet *viçvárūpa* serves to emphasize the reference to the light,[4] he is said to

[1] X. 17. 1, 2.
[2] Compare V. 43. 6. with VII. 34. 21.
[3] III. 4. 9., VII. 34. 20., X. 184. 1.; I. 188. 9.; X. 64. 10.
[4] See Grassmann's Lex. s.v.; cf. Chānd. Up. 5. 13. 1.

have nourished and given birth to all existing things. Further, the same name appears to be used interchangeably with that of Gandharva for the father of Yama and Yamī; and Tvashṭar receives the epithet *agriyá*, the first-born.[1] We have thus arrived at the following complication in the matrimonial relations of the sun-gods: Gandharva, Agni, Soma, Pūshan, Tvashṭar, and Vivasvat are all represented as the bridegrooms of Sūryā, the daughter of the sun, or of Saraṇyū, the daughter of Tvashṭar. The Ṛishis were not, however, content with the attainment of this bizarre result of their symbolisms; they delight in describing the complication in its most paradoxical form, that the father married his own daughter, and with her gave birth to the universe.[2] We are thus brought back to the point from which we started, the union of the light with the waters confused with the marriage of the sun, the first-born, with the dawn, and regarded as the type of generation in the world.

We now proceed to the discussion of the principal hymns, among the most difficult in the Ṛigveda, in which the figurative generation of the world is described. The first hymn X. 72. contains the barest outlines of a cosmogony, the details of which remain in obscurity. There are two interpolations

[1] X. 10. 5.; I. 13. 10.

[2] V. 42. 13., and especially X. 61., I. 164. 33.

in the hymn (verses 2, and 6, 7); the original verses, which are especially closely connected together, admit more readily than in most hymns of separation from the interpolations.

1. "Let us now proclaim with admiration the births of the gods, in utterances of praise, that a man may hear them (lit. see) in a later age.[1]

3. In the first age of the gods the existent was born from the non-existent; after that the regions (of the sky) were born from the begetter (the sky).[2]

4. The earth was born from the begetter, the regions (of the earth) from the earth. From Aditi Daksha was born, and again from Daksha Aditi.

5. Even Aditi had a birth, for she is thy daughter, Daksha; after her the blessed gods were born, of immortal parentage.

8. Eight in number are the sons which were born of Aditi, from her body; she went forth to meet the gods with seven, and cast the bird (Mārtāṇḍa) away.[3]

9. With seven sons Aditi went forth to meet the

[1] For *paç* in the sense of 'hear,' cf. X. 71. 4. Or we may translate with Delbrück, Altindische Tempuslehre, p. 14, 'whoever' or 'as one who seeth in a later age.' For the construction cf. VIII. 6. 18.

[2] The meaning of the *ἅπ. εἰρ.* *uttānápadaḥ* is quite uncertain; *uttāná* is used as an epithet of *bhū́mi*, but this proves nothing for *uttānápad*. If we take the word as masculine, and refer it to the sky, we obtain with *bhū́* a pair corresponding to Daksha and Aditi in the next two verses.

[3] "The exposure of Mārtāṇḍa (Sūrya) refers apparently only to his sweeping through the sky (*upári prā́kshipat*)."—Ludwig.

earliest age, she brought the bird thither to be born and die again."

The interpolated verses are—

2. "Brahmaṇaspati welded these worlds together like a smith; in the earliest age of the gods the existent was born from the non-existent" (cf. X. 81. 3.).

6. "When ye, O gods, stood firmly embracing one another in the formless depth, thence there arose from your feet a thickening volume of dust as from dancers.

7. When ye, O gods, like the Yatis, made all things to grow, then ye brought forward the sun, which was hidden in the sea."

The two verses 6 and 7 are interesting as containing an independent story of the origin of the world: the gods are said to have kicked up in dancing the atoms which formed the earth. We may also notice the usual mention of the production of the sun as soon as heaven and earth were made. The nearest parallel to this passage in the Ṛigveda is X. 24. 4, 5., addressed to the Açvins: "You two strong and cunning ones produced by churning (as with a fire-drill) the two (worlds) that face one another. When, O Nāsatyā (Açvins), worshipped by Vimada, ye produced them by churning, all the gods yearned as the two (worlds) facing one another fell away. 'O Nāsatyā,' spake the gods, 'bring them here again.'" Apparently the Açvins stirred up the dust, which formed heaven and earth, and the gods were so pleased with the production that they wished to have them formed into solid masses.[1] Similarly in I. 22. 17. the earth seems to have been formed from the dust of Vishṇu's three strides across the heavens. The passages are, however, too isolated to admit of anything more than conjectures; we return to the body of the hymn.

The mention of the non-existent and the existent merely introduces the subject of origins, as will be shown at the end of this chapter. The hymn contains three moments; first, the birth of the three worlds, heaven, earth, and the intermediate regions; next, parallel to the birth of the worlds, the birth of the gods from their first parents; lastly, the rise and setting of the sun, represented by the figure of Mārtāṇḍa. That *mārtāṇḍá* has the meaning 'bird' is proved by II. 38. 8.; the word is perhaps here chosen in allusion to the semi-divinity and semi-mortality of the rising and setting sun. The relation of Aditi to Daksha remains to be discussed. The general meaning of the word *dáksha* is 'active energy'; it is applied three times to the Ṛibhus; it is used of the production of hymns at the sacrifice; it is opposed to sickness; and occasionally it has the sense of malevolent activity. The personification of Daksha as well as of Aditi is most probably to be traced in the hymns themselves to an old idiom of

[1] cf. Ait. Br. IV. 4. 27.

the Vedic language. In VIII. 25. 5. Mitra and Varuṇa are called "the children of strength, and the sons of *dáksha*," i.e. the strong and active ones. The expressions are common, and translators are agreed as to their meaning. We find now that the description of Indra as 'son of strength,' gave rise to the conception of a goddess Çavasī, his mother;[1] and it is scarcely less certain that Daksha, an unimportant deity whose only characteristic in the Ṛigveda is his fatherhood of the gods, has derived his personality from similar expressions.[2] The analogy of these two figures suggests at once a like explanation of the origin of the motherhood of Aditi. The motherhood of the gods is the only constant and certain attribute of Aditi. Aditi and Daksha are mentioned together again in X. 5. 7. and 64. 5., a recurrence which confirms the derivation of both from a like origin. The history of the word may have been somewhat as follows. It was used in pre-vedic times as an abstract word meaning 'freedom from bondage,' if the generally accepted etymology be correct. The determination of the sons of Aditi as a class of gods was caused by the association of the expression with particular gods. The *áditeḥ putrā́ḥ*, 'the unfettered gods,' became the sons of Aditi, and from this later sense the name Āditya was derived. There is no proof

[1] *putrā́ḥ çávasaḥ* VIII. 92. 14.; *çávasaḥ sūnúḥ* IV. 24. 1.; Çavasī X. 153. 2. cf. note 1 on page 31.

[2] v. s. v. *dákshapitar* Pet. Lex. cf. IX. 87. 2.

that at the time when our hymns were composed the word still bore the supposed etymological meaning of 'freedom from bondage.' It is used as an adjective and as a substantive in so many and varied connexions that no single conception has yet been proposed sufficiently elastic to suit all its applications. The ambiguity of meaning will be explained if we suppose that after the word had become a proper name it was employed anew, in the same way and in much the same sense as the appellative *ásura,* with a vague sense of a grand divine significance.[1] In IX. 74. 5. it is Soma who placed the fruit in Aditi's womb, through which we obtain children and grandchildren.

The next passage which will occupy our attention is a fragment, X. 31. 7–10. Whether it come from the same poet who wrote the preceding six verses of the hymn or no, the connection of thought is sufficiently loose for us to treat these four verses alone. The subject is the first birth of the sun.

[1] A collection of passages will be found in Professor A. Hillebrandt's monograph, Ueber die Göttin Aditi, Breslau, 1876. The parallelism of *áditi* and *ásura* is seen in the application of both words principally to persons (Hillebrandt, *l.c.* p. 15): in the similarity of the derivatives from the two words, *adititvá* and *asuratvá*, *ādityá* and *āsurá*, *díti* and *súra*: and in such passages as IV. 1. 20. compared with III. 3. 4.; V. 44. 11. with X. 74. 2.; VII. 51. 1. with X. 50. 3.; I. 89. 10. with VI. 36. 1.; V. 59. 8., X. 63. 3. with I. 131. 1.; cf. also X. 67. 2., X. 10. 2. As *áditi* is the cow, so *ásura* is in III. 38. 4. and V. 12. 1. an epithet of *vṛíshan.* The fluctuating attributes of the goddess Aditi, as distinguished from those attributes which are derived from her motherhood, are, for the most part, borrowed directly from the Ādityas.

"7. What indeed was the wood? What too was that tree, from which they fashioned the heaven and the earth? They two stand fast and grow not old for ever, while many days and mornings wax old.

8. There is no other thing besides like unto him; he is the bull that beareth heaven and earth; of his own power he maketh his skin a source of light,[1] when the bay horses carry him as the sun.

9. As a Stega over the ground so he passeth over the earth;[2] he penetrateth the world, as the wind scattering a mist; there, where Mitra and Varuṇa are, he when anointed hath shot abroad his light, as Agni in the wood (*i.e.* at sacrifice).

10. When the barren cow (the earth) beareth, immediately on being anointed she maketh her insecure paths secure (at daybreak), who hath her own herdsman (or herself her own herdsman); when the first son is born from his parents, the cow devoureth the placenta (?) which they seek."[3]

The verses deal with the formation of the three

[1] Compare *súryatvac.* The Pet. Lex. translates *pavitra* 'sieve.' It would then signify the filter through which the beams of the sun stream. The literal meaning of the word is 'instrument of illumination or purification.' A similar passage is I. 160. 3.

[2] Thus the grammatical parallelism of the first and second pādas is complete. The Stega is a biting or stinging insect.

[3] The sense of *vyáthiḥ* in all passages is 'an insecure going.' For our passage cf. II. 35. 5., II. 4. 7. The Pet. Lex. and Grassmann take the word *çamyā́m* as equivalent to *çámyām*, 'a plug or peg.' The original reading may possibly have been some such word as *jarā́yu* (? *çámalam*),

main components of the universe, heaven, earth, and the sun. Of the first two the poet has little to tell us, and passes on at once to the third. The sun is identified with the bull, Agni of the sacrifice, and the earth with the lower rubbing-stick anointed with ghee, which is licked up as soon as fire is struck.

The next hymn is again a description of the rise of the sun, his birth in the east; the cosmogonic significance of the hymn does not appear till the last verse, which may be regarded as the climax of the whole, or may be but an afterthought. The allusions do not admit of certain explanation. I add the interpretations which seem to me the most plausible.

X. 5. 1. "The one sea (the sun) bearing rich treasures, producing many births, is to us all a sight of gladness. He sucketh the teat on the breast of his hidden parents; in the midst of the fount (source of light in the East) is placed the home of the bird.

2. The strong, lusty horses dwelling in a common stall come together with the mares (light and waters). The wise (the rays, see Chapter III.) guard the home of nature's order, they assume excellent forms in secret.

3. The two cunning ones (heaven and earth) who

which would yield a suitable antecedent to *ydd* and give an intelligible sense, cf. A. V. VI. 49. 1. With *stari̍r ydd sū́ta* compare VII. 101. 3. *stari̍r u tvad bhávati, sū́ta u tvat,* where the reference to the earth is still clearer.

follow nature's order unite; they form and give birth to the child, nourishing him, the centre of all that is fixed and that moveth, weaving[1] with insight the thread of the wise.

4. For the tracks of nature's course and the juices (dews and light) for refreshment follow the goodly child from of old; heaven and earth, clothing themselves in a mantle, are strengthened by the rich nourishment of the sweet drink.

5. His seven glowing sisters (rays and waters) as a lover the understanding one bringeth forth from the sweet drink to be seen; he who is of ancient birth halteth in the sky, and seeking hath found the dome of heaven.[2]

6. The (seven) wise ones (rays) fashion seven lines, to one of these may the distressed mortal come.[3] The support of life in the home of the highest, at the divergence of the ways, standeth on sure ground.

[1] Read *váyantī*, cf. II. 3. 6. For the thought compare VI. 9.

[2] The rendering of *vavrím pūshaṇásya* is a paraphrase. The context leads us to expect an expression of the journey of the sun up towards the zenith. The word *pūshaṇá* is an ἅπ. εἰρ. If we retain the text as it stands, Pūshan's covering will be probably the sphere of his movement. For *vavrí* compare IV. 42. 1. and X. 4. 4.

[3] The 'distressed' one, lit. 'compressed,' is the mortal longing for daybreak. The 'lines' *maryádāḥ* are the beams of light; the word occurs again in IV. 5. 13. along with *vayúnā* (pl.), a word with a similar development of meaning; compare also *saptáraçmin*. These beams diverge as paths from the point where the sun stands, I. 46. 11. When the sun is just rising there are two paths, the dark and the light, III. 55. 15. Ludwig renders the word here 'ways,' but assigns to it a moral significance following Sāyana.

7. The non-existent and the existent are in highest heaven in the birthplace of Daksha, in Aditi's lap. Agni is our firstborn of nature's order, and in the beginning of life a lusty bull."

In the next hymn a sun-god is glorified as the great power of the universe, from which all other powers and existences, divine and earthly, are derived, a conception which is the nearest approach to the later mystical conception of Brahmā, the creator of the world. The hymn is addressed to Hiraṇyagarbha, the gold-germ, who in the last verse is addressed as Prajāpati, the prototype and lord of things born. The name Hiraṇyagarbha marks the association of the conception with the light; the other references to the sun in the hymn are equally clear; but the god is already beginning to be abstracted into an independent figure, though tentatively as appears from the refrain.

X. 121. 1.[1] "Hiraṇyagarbha (gold-germ) was formed in the beginning; when born he was the sole lord of being. He holdeth fast the heaven here and the earth; what god shall we honour with sacrifice?[2]

2. Who giveth breath and giveth strength; whose prescriptions all the gods perform; whose (light and) shadow is immortality and death;[3] what god shall we honour with sacrifice?

[1] Translated by Prof. Max Müller, Hibbert Lectures, p. 295.

[2] A similar phrase occurs in X. 168. 4., VIII. 48. 13.

[3] Ludwig translates *chāyā́* here 'Glanz,' Grassmann 'Schattenbild.'

3. Who by his power is become sole king of the living world, that breatheth and slumbereth; who ruleth over its men and beasts; what god shall we honour with sacrifice?

4. Who by his power, they tell us, possesseth these snowy mountains, and the sea with the Rasā (a mythical river); whose arms are these regions; what god shall we honour with sacrifice?

5. Through whom the strong heaven and the earth are made secure,[1] through whom the realm of light is supported, and the vault of the sky, who traverseth the air in the middle region; what god shall we honour with sacrifice?

6. To whom the two battle-hosts, sustained by his support, looked up as they trembled in spirit, there where the risen sun shines;[2] what god shall we honour with sacrifice?

7. When the august waters went, receiving the germ of all and producing fire; thence arose the living spirit of the gods [which is one];[3] what god shall we honour with sacrifice?

8. Who surveyed with power the mighty waters, when they received productive energy (*dáksha*) and

[1] Ludwig and Grassmann take *ugrā́* as a predicate: but in that construction the sense of the word 'actively strong, fresh,' makes a poor parallel to *dṛiḷhā́* and *stabhitám*.

[2] The battle begins at dawn. The expression is applied to Indra in II. 12. 8. Dadhikrā, the rising sun in the form of a war-horse, is similarly invoked by contending armies; IV. 38. 5., 39. 5.

[3] Two syllables extra; *ékaḥ* is suspicious.

begat sacrifice; who alone is god over the gods; what god shall we honour with sacrifice?

9. Let not the begetter of the earth harm us, nor he who hath begotten the heaven, whose ordinance is sure, who hath begotten the mighty and shining waters; what god shall we honour with sacrifice?

[10. Prajāpati, no other than thou is become lord over all these productions; grant us our desire when we call upon thee; may we be possessors of wealth.]"[1]

The hymn is an enumeration by a wearisome repetition of the relative pronoun of the general characteristics of a great god. We look, therefore, for the most special attributes in the first few verses. Hiraṇyagarbha, 'the gold-germ,' is born in the beginning, giving life and strength, typifying life and death, king of the breathing and slumbering world, whose arms are the regions of the sky. In other passages Prajāpati is invoked for fruitful increase of children, or of cattle, and once he is identified with Soma.[2] Savitar also receives the title *bhúvanasya prajā́patiḥ,* 'the prajāpati of the world.' It could not be expected that such a conception as that of

[1] The last verse is not divided up in the pada recension; this fact and the absence of the refrain would seem to prove the verse a later addition. Grassmann is not therefore strictly correct in describing the hymn as addressed to Prajāpati, and treating *hiraṇyagarbhá* as a mere appellative. Later mythology would incline us to discover in Hiraṇyagarbha a reference to the mythical primeval egg; there is, however, no passage in the Ṛigveda, except perhaps I. 130. 3., to support such a reference.

[2] X. 85. 43., 184. 1., 169. 4.; IX. 5. 9.

Hiraṇyagarbha would be limited to the sun, and indeed in later times the connection with the sun sank into obscurity; but that this connection was as vividly present to the minds of the poets as in the case of Savitar is established by this hymn and the references to Prajāpati which have been cited. The following passages will further show that, independently of this name, the sun was in process of elevation to the position of supreme and only god which was afterwards occupied by Brahmā, the creator. In I. 115. 1. the sun is called "the life (*ātmán*) of all that moveth and standeth." "They call it Indra, Mitra, Varuṇa, Agni, and it is the strong-winged bird (Garutmat) of the sky; though it is one (*ékaṁ sát*), the poets address it in many ways; they call it Agni, Yama, and Mātariçvan." "The wise singers in their utterances ascribe to the strong-winged bird, which is but one (*ékaṁ sántam*), many forms."[1]

We have thus seen the sun not only figure as the main type and agent of generation in the world, but, owing to the important place which it occupies in cosmological speculations, even regarded as the most divine of all the gods, embracing in himself their most godlike functions and attributes, including the attribute of creator. The next step was easily taken. As he was the first of things born, so he

[1] I. 164. 46., X. 114. 5., cf. V. 3. 1., 13. 6., Vāl. 10. 2.

is represented as the Unborn (*ajá*). The characteristic creative functions of Aja, the Unborn, are indicated to us in two passages in the clearest manner in which characteristic functions can be indicated, that is to say, by comparison of other gods with him. In I. 67. 5. Agni is said to have made fast the earth, like the Unborn, to have supported the sky with effective utterances. In VIII. 41. 10. it is Varuṇa who "measured out the ancient dwelling-place, and made heaven and earth fast, and the sky with a support like the Unborn." The hymn to Hiraṇya-garbha supplies us also with a clue to the next two passages. "It rested on the navel of the Unborn, that alone (*ékam*) in which all existing things abide;" "he who supported these six regions of the air in the form of the Unborn, what is that one?"[1]

It was stated at the beginning of this chapter that the element fire was not regarded in the Ṛigveda as a material out of which the world was made. This is the more striking when we consider how large a proportion of the book is directly addressed to Agni in his varied character as embodying the different kinds of fire and light. The passages which

[1] X. 82. 6., I. 164. 6. If this Aja is to be identified with Aja Ekapād, in X. 65. 13. the bearer of heaven, the ascription of one foot to the sun might be due to his appearance alone in the sky as opposed to the dawns and the Açvins, cf. VIII. 41. 8. His association with Ahi Budhnya would then be accounted for by the play on the word *ajá*, 'goat.'

approach nearest to a cosmogonic significance are those in which Agni shows most clearly the side of his character which represents the light and warmth of the sun. He is said to place the embryo in existing things; or he is himself the embryo of the waters, of the trees, of things standing still and moving; he places the germ in plants and in all things existing, he produces generation on the earth and in women; he enters the plants, and mounts up in them; he is the herdsman of the nations, the generator of the worlds and all existing things are offshoots from him.[1] There is, however, one passage which would appear to approach very near to the conception of fire and water as primary elements. The Ṛibhus are represented as speaking 'correct' words when forming the cups: "'The waters are most excellent,' said one; 'fire is most excellent,' said another; the third praised the thunderbolt (or the cloud containing the lightning) exceedingly."[2] The translation is not certain and the meaning too obscure to admit of any inference as to the allusions in the sayings. In another passage a Ṛishi propounds the question, "how many fires, dawns, and suns are there?" and assures the wise fathers in heaven that he is not putting the question as a riddle, but really seeking for information.[3]

[1] III. 2. 10, 11.; I. 70. 3.; X. 183. 3., cf. III. 56. 3., IV. 58. 5.; I. 98. 2., I. 67. 9.; II. 35. 8.

[2] I. 161. 9.

[3] X. 88. 18.

We come now to the waters. They figure alone as the mothers; the streams, and in particular the Sindhu, are the most motherly of mothers.[1] They know the birth of heaven and earth; they are the begetters of all that stands and moves; they are the mothers and wives of the existing world, growing up together in one home.[2] Their cosmogonic activity is, however, much more frequently described in union with the light in such passages as those already quoted. The origin of the world is conceived on the analogy of the common experience of ordinary life. The advance of the sun into the watery heaven and the shooting of the lightning from the dark masses of the rain-clouds are the signs of the periodic regeneration of the world; Rudra, the storm-god, is the divine physician, and the waters are his vivifying medicines; the origin of the world was, therefore, held to have been due to a primeval sunrise or a primeval thunderstorm.[3] The light was the first germ, the waters were the bearers of the germ.[4]

The general fructifying agency of the storm, which is so all-important in India, finds its clearest expression in the figure of Parjanya, the god of the rain-cloud. He is the god who fructifies the earth as a rutting bull; he produces fruit in plants, mares, cows, and

[1] VIII. 78. 4., I. 158. 5., III. 33. 3.
[2] VII. 34. 2., VI. 50. 7., X. 30. 10.
[3] Cf. *e.g.* Vāl. 3. 8.
[4] Cf. X. 82. 1.

women; and hence receives the title of father.[1] The Maruts similarly receive the title because they, as a husband, place the fructifying germ in the earth and in women.[2] "Parjanya produceth rain, Agni the embryo; may ye both give us strength to beget children."[3] The following hymn describes the most characteristic actions of Parjanya.

VII. 101. 1. "Speak the three words that are pointed with light,[4] which milk this udder of sweet milk; as soon as the bull is born he belloweth, producing calves and the germ in plants.

2. He who giveth increase of plants and waters, who ruleth as god over the living world; may he grant threefold protection and shelter, and threefold light for our assistance.

3. Now she is barren and now she bringeth forth, he formeth her body as it may please him; the mother receiveth milk from the father; thereby is the father strengthened and also the son.[5]

4. In whom all things abide; through the three heavens threefold the waters flow: the three dripping vats flow with mead on all sides plentifully.

[1] V. 83. 1, 6., VII. 102. 2., VII. 101. 3.

[2] VI. 49. 10., V. 58. 7., X. 63. 15., V. 53. 13.

[3] VI. 52. 16.

[4] Perhaps with reference to the comparison of the sacrificial prayers to the arrow-like flames of the sacrificial fire, cf. X. 87. 4., II. 24. 8. Mention of the *tisró vâcaḥ* recurs in IX. 97. 34., cf. VII. 33. 7.

[5] His wife is the earth, cf. A. V. XII. 1. 12.; the sun is probably the lightning of IX. 82. 3.

5. May this hymn please Parjanya, the monarch, may he accept it favourably; may quickening rain be ours, and fruitful plants tended by the god.

6. He is the fructifying bull of the multitude of maidens (waters cf. III. 56. 3.), in him is the breath of all that moveth and standeth; may this sacrifice protect me for a thousand years—protect us ever, ye gods, with blessings."

The principle of cosmogonic generation was, however, already in the Ṛigveda extended beyond the union of the light and the waters. We find mention in one hymn of a primordial substance or unit out of which the universe was developed. This is 'the one thing' (*ékam*) which we have already met with in connection with Aja, the Unborn,[1] and which is also used synonymously with the universe[2] in accordance with the principle which is the key to much of the later mysticism that cause and effect are identical. The poet endeavours in a strain, which preludes the philosophy of the Upanishads, to picture to himself the first state of the world, and the first signs of life and growth in it. The speculations of the Veda are, however, characterized by a marked difference of tone as compared with those of the Upanishads in the absence in them of the practical end and object of the latter, deliverance from the world.

[1] I. 164. 6, 46., X. 82. 6.

[2] III. 54. 8., X. 48. 7., Vāl. 10. 2.

X. 129. 1.[1] "The non-existent was not, and the existent was not at that time; there was no air nor sky beyond; what was the covering in? and where? under shelter of what? was there water—a deep depth?

2. Death was not nor immortality then, there was no discrimination[2] of night and day: that one thing breathed without a wind of its own self; apart from it there was nothing else at all beyond.

3. Darkness there was, hidden in darkness, in the beginning, everything here was an indiscriminate chaos; it was void covered with emptiness, all that was; that one thing was born by the power of warmth.

4. So in the beginning arose desire, which was the first seed of mind; the wise found out by thought, searching in the heart, the parentage of the existent in the non-existent.

5. Their line was stretched across; what was above? what was below? there were generators, there were mighty powers; *svadhá* below, the presentation of offerings above.

6. Who knoweth it forsooth? who can announce

[1] The latest of the many commentators on this hymn are Professor Whitney in the Journal of the American Oriental Society, vol. xi. p. cix, and Dr. Schermann, Philosophische Hymnen aus der Ṛig- und Atharva-Veda-Saṁhitā verglichen mit den Philosophemen der älteren Upanishads, 1887.

[2] Or *praketá* may perhaps have here the sense of 'light-giver, illuminator,' which would also be suitable in I. 113. 1. and I. 94. 5. We should then translate in verse 2. 'there was no light of the day nor of the night,' and in verse 3. 'all this was a lightless chaos.'

it here (= III. 54. 5.)? whence it was born, whence this creation is. The gods came by the creating of it (*i.e.* the one thing); who then knoweth whence it is come into being?

7. Whence this creation (lit. emission) is come into being, whether it was ordained or no—he whose eye is over all in the highest heaven, he indeed knoweth it, or may be he knoweth it not."

If we accept the text as it stands, *eshām* 'their' in verse 5 will refer to *kavāyaḥ*, 'the wise.' 'Their line' is a beam of their light. The word *prāyati* in the other passages where it occurs has only the meaning 'presentation of sacrifice'; if we retain this meaning and the allusion to the ancient fathers, technically expressed by the word *svadhā́*,[1] we obtain a natural parallel to the contrast of the preceding pāda between *retodhā́ḥ* and *mahimā́naḥ* in the free action or enjoyment of the fathers below and the sacrifice of the gods above. The chief difficulty which presented itself to the mind of the poet was to make a division between the upper world and the lower, to bring dualism out of unity: it is for this purpose that he introduces 'the wise,' who draw their line across, dividing heaven and earth. This solution, however, failed to satisfy him, and he gives

[1] The primary meaning of *svadhā́* is 'free action according to the unfettered will of the actor;' accordingly it is used of the happiness of the fathers: *dhā* has in the compound almost the sense of our *do*, as in *éno dádhānaḥ* II. 12. 10., *aghásya dhātā́* I. 123. 5.

up the problem in despair. The principle of generation, on the other hand, underlies the whole as a self-evident principle of cosmogony: desire (*káma*, ἔρως) is the first requisite of generation; it is the seed of thought; the wise find the *bándhu*, 'relationship' or 'parentage' of the existent in the non-existent; the fathers are represented as *retodhā́ḥ*, the generators. Hence the translation 'warmth' is preferable to 'asceticism' for *tápas*; the warmth explains how the process of birth became possible.[1] The hymn is remarkable for the clearness of expression of the automatic evolution of the world; the universe is represented as emanating of itself from the one thing, like a stream issuing from a fountain-head.

Lastly we come to the expressions *ásat* and *sát*, the 'non-existent' and the 'existent.' The word *ásat* is used in the Ṛigveda in two senses, as an adjective with *vácas* 'speech' and as the converse of *sát* as in the passage before us. In the first case the meaning is clear; it is equivalent to *asatyá*,

[1] cf. X. 190. 1. The question as to the relation of *kā́ma* and *tápas* in these verses to the later *tápo 'tapyata* and *só 'kāmayata* of the Brāhmaṇas is a part of the general question of the relation of the Ṛigveda to the Brāhmaṇas. The cosmological importance of warmth in the view of the ancient Āryas receives a full treatment in M. Emile Burnouf's La Science des Religions, pp. 207 ff. "Trois phénomènes ont frappé l'intelligence des Āryas, dès le temps où ils n'habitaient encore que les vallées de l'Oxus: ce sont le *mouvement*, la *vie* et la *pensée*. Ces trois choses, prises dans leur étendue, embrassent tous les phénomènes naturels sans exception." He proceeds to show how *warmth* was regarded as the principle explaining all three forms of action.

the unreal or the false, the converse of that which is really the fact.[1] When used with *sát* it occurs invariably in passages of a cosmogonic character; *sát* is said to be born from *ásat*, that is, translated into modern idiom, *ásat* precedes *sát* or *ásat* becomes *sát*; we are told that Indra made *ásat* into *sát* in a trice; or *ásat* and *sát* are mentioned as in our hymn as belonging to the first creation.[2] Where the two words are coupled together by a conjunction, *ásat* always precedes *sát*. The *ásat* must therefore have had in itself the potentiality of existence; it is not merely the 'non-existent,' but may almost be translated the 'not yet existing,' as *bhávat* is elsewhere opposed to *sát*,[3] *jáyamānam* to *jātám*, and *bhávyam* to *bhūtám*. It is not colourless as our word 'nothing,' it is the negation of *sát*. Thus the whole meaning expressed by these dark words is nothing more than the process of becoming, the beginning of development or creation.

The subject of this chapter is of special interest as illustrating the relation between the symbolical

[1] V. 12. 4., VII. 104. 8, 12, 13. cf. *ásatā* IV. 5. 14.

[2] X. 72. 1, 2., VI. 24. 5., X. 5. 7. The philosophic comment of Sāyana on verse X. 129. 1. is disproved by the expression *sató bándhum ásati nír avindan* in verse 4. If we treat the hymn philosophically, we must assume a stage between those states described in verses 1 and 4 in which *ásat* was present, but there was as yet no *sát*. The context, however, shows that the poet merely wished to shadow forth a condition in which absolutely nothing existed; and the presence of *ásat* is denied because it was inseparably associated with *sát*.

[3] I. 96. 7., A. V. VII. 1. 19.

or allegorical manner of thought, which is an important factor in the formation of mythology, and the analogical or metaphorical method of early speculation. In the one case forces and agencies are clothed with a distinct personality, they are endowed in some measure with an active will and character; in the other the actions only are viewed as partaking of the nature of human actions. The poets of our hymns feel themselves less constrained to analyse the processes of creation, the mode of working of the different productive forces, than to define and specify the nature of the agents. The nouns—to borrow the phraseology of grammar—lose their anthropomorphism sooner than the verbs. The two metaphors which have now been passed in review, the metaphor of building and that of generation, are used almost indiscriminately to express the action of any creative agent; and in the following chapters we shall meet with no further attempt to elucidate the process of creation.

CHAPTER III.

THE SACRIFICE.

In the explanations of the origin of the world which were described in the two preceding chapters there was room for considerable difference of opinion as to the extent to which they were influenced by the sacrificial system of the Ṛishis. The theory which is the subject for consideration in this chapter may be regarded as specially characteristic of the Ṛishis. In the former cases it was natural to assume that the motive of speculation was the desire to discover a plausible explanation of the origin of things; in the present case we are unable to decide whether the motive was purely speculative or the outcome of the exigencies of a system. The glorification of the sacrifice, which was the main task of the Ṛishis, led them to represent the sacrifice in the light of the supreme cause of all successful action in the world, and it may have been only in consequence of this representation that they extended its working to the creation and ordering of the universe.

The sacrifice, as it appears in the Ṛigveda, is the means of gratifying a god by ministering to his wants, and so enabling him to perform his wonted actions; it is an instrument through which a relation of mutual friendship between a god and his worshippers is established. The later idea of the sacrifice as a contract between a man and his god, which could be used against a god to force him to perform the will of the sacrificer, does not find expression in our hymns. Those passages in the Ṛigveda, which through the omission of the mention of the gods might seem to ascribe to the sacrifice in the hands of man a power independent of the gods, can in all cases be explained either as referring to divine sacrificers, or as assuming the co-operation of the gods. On the other hand, human sacrificers are represented as associating themselves with the gods through the sacrifice, as assisting the gods in their actions, and in an after-life or in a state of ecstasy as participating in divine power. The worship of deceased ancestors is well known to be one of the very earliest forms of worship, traces of which survive in every popular form of religion. The Ṛigveda allows us in this particular to draw an unusually clear line of distinction between the common conceptions of death as they existed in the minds of the people, and the peculiar colouring given to them by the bias of the Vedic Ṛishis.

According to the popular view, the first ancestor who died, the king of the land of the dead, is Yama. One passage added on to the last hymn but one of the ninth book, where it is entirely out of place as if inserted with a careless contempt of its contents, gives us a description of the happy land of the dead in the third heaven, where Yama reigns as king in perfect bliss. It is a land of undimmed brightness, "where bliss and rejoicings, joy, exceeding joy are to be found, where all wishes are fulfilled; there," prays the poet, "make me immortal."[1] In another hymn Yama is represented as revelling on a tree of goodly foliage, "the father, lord of the people, showing favour to our ancestors." The fathers found this home of the blessed by following his footsteps past the dreadful watch-dogs, and he prepares a place there for the dead in Vishṇu's realm of light.[2]

According to the Ṛishis, existence after death and the superhuman power of the fathers depend upon the due performance of the sacrifice; immortality is said to be conferred upon the priests by a sacrificial god; for the patrons of the sacrifice it is the reward of liberality.[3] Yama, on the other hand, the ancient popular deity, is not primarily a sacrificer.[4] The position of the fathers, the ancestors of the Ṛishis, in the spirit-world, is that of a partnership with the gods. Indra is "the maintainer of the

[1] IX. 113. 7–11.

[2] X. 135. 1., X. 14. 2., X. 18. 13., I. 154. 5.

[3] VI. 1. 4., I. 31. 7.; I. 125. 5, 6., X. 107. 2.

[4] A figure in many respects analogous to Yama is that of Trita, who is represented as an ancient primeval warrior, and whose connection with the sacrifice is limited to the pressing of soma.

poets, the friend of the fathers in old time."[1] "They were banqueters with the gods, the wise men of old, who observed the sacred order; the fathers found the hidden light, with effective utterances they begat the dawn."[2] They are associated with different gods as friends or assistants in carrying out their characteristic works. In particular they assist Indra in his battle with the demons, when he sets free the cows of light and rain, even supplying him with his weapon the thunderbolt.[3] It is in agreement with the gods and fathers that Prajāpati gives increase in cattle.[4] In this particular they occupy a similar position to Bṛihaspati, or Brahmaṇaspati, the lord of the sacrificial prayer, who is also Indra's assistant, and figures in very many passages along with the ancient Ṛishis who are called his sons. But the alliance with Indra is not confined to the deified sacrificers; the priests on earth also associate themselves with him in his combats, and supply him with the thunderbolt to strike the demons. "I and thou, O slayer of Vṛitra," exclaims one bold Ṛishi, "will unite for victory."[5] In X. 120. 9. the poet, Bṛihaddeva, even identifies himself with Indra.

More striking and significant is the relation of

[1] VI. 21. 8., cf. VII. 33. 4.
[2] VII. 76. 4.
[3] I. 121. 12., II. 11. 4,
[4] X. 196. 4.
[5] X. 44. 9., V. 30. 8., VIII. 62. 11., cf. VIII. 69. 7, 16.

the ancient fathers to Agni, based perhaps on an earlier sun-worship. The familiar mythical conception of the origin of the human race from fire becomes to the Ṛishis the origin of the ancestral sacrificers from Agni. Agni, as also other gods of the light, the Açvins and the Ādityas,[1] is the blood-relative of the fathers, and of the sacrificing priest himself; he is their father, and himself a father, in the technical sense, the friend of the fathers, the most fatherly father.[2] The connection with Agni is so close that the fathers are even identified with the rays of Agni's light,[3] which are not regarded as inherent in the sun, the lightning or the fire, but as apportioned to them by the gods.[4] "It is these beams of the sun with which our fathers were united, O Indra and Agni."[5] The rays are mystically represented as seven in number, parallel to the seven rivers of heaven and earth; the seven ancient Ṛishis are the seven friends of Agni, his seven horses, or seven heads.[6]

This connection of the fathers with the light, of

[1] III. 54. 16., II. 29. 3, 4.

[2] I. 31. 10., IV. 17. 17., et passim.

[3] I. 115. 2., cf. Çat. Br. I. 9. 3. 10.

[4] *e.g.* X. 12. 7., cf. III. 2. 12.

[5] I. 109. 7.

[6] A very frequent designation of the fathers as ancient sacrificers is *náraḥ*. The identification of the fathers with the rays of light may perhaps explain the difficult words *nṛicákshas* 'who is the sight of *men*,' and *vaiçvānará* 'who embraces all *men*,' both primarily attributes of Agni or the sun; compare especially III. 2. 12., 14. 4., I. 146. 4., X. 45. 3.

which they are both the embodiments and the guardians,[1] is alone sufficient to explain their action in placing the stars in the sky: "the fathers adorned the sky with stars as a black horse with jewels; they gave darkness to the night and light to the day."[2] Indra and Atri, an ancestor of sacrificers, free the sun from the demon who causes eclipses.[3] Since light is the type of wisdom and knowledge,[4] the fathers are regarded as especially endowed with divine insight, and it is particularly as the rays of light that they receive the appellative 'the wise' (*kaváyaḥ*).[5]

The general character of the fathers will be best illustrated by a consideration of the most important family of priestly fathers that finds mention in the Ṛigveda, the family of the Aṅgirases. Their association with the light is so pronounced that Professor Roth (Pet. Lex.) defines them as a race of higher beings between gods and men, and regards their priestly character as a later development. Professor Weber conjectures that they were originally the priests of the earlier common religion of the Indians and Persians.[6] The following description will limit

[1] X. 154. 5.
[2] X. 68. 11., cf. I. 68. 10.
[3] V. 40. 6–8.
[4] cf. III. 1. 5.
[5] I. 164. 5., X. 88., I. 185. 1., X. 5.
[6] Indische Studien, vol. i. p. 291.

itself to the conception of the Añgirases held by the Ṛishis themselves. They are regarded as the typical first sacrificers, whose ritual is the pattern which later priests must follow; hence the frequent expression "after the manner of the Añgirases."[1] By the offering of sacrifice they obtained Indra's friendship and immortality (X. 62. 1.); they became the sons of the gods;[2] Bṛihaspati is himself called an Añgiras. For them Indra is said to have recovered the cows and slain the demon Vala; or again, it was after he had been worshipped by them that he was able to achieve his victories.[3] The poet of VI. 18. 5. prays for such a friendship with Indra, as that in which he was praised by the Añgirases and smote the demon. On the other hand, Indra is mentioned as himself their leader, the most Añgiras-like, with the Añgirases;[4] or his name is omitted and his characteristic actions are attributed directly to the Añgirases.[5] They give gifts like Mitra and Bhaga, and are invoked along with the gods; they set the sun on high and spread out the earth.[6]

Agni is similarly the best or oldest of the Añgirases;[7] he is the first Añgiras, the Ṛishi,

[1] *e.g.* I. 31. 17., 139. 9.
[2] *devâputrā ṛishayaḥ* X. 62. 1, 4.
[3] I. 132. 4., VIII. 14. 8., 63. 3.; I. 62. 5., X. 111. 4.
[4] I. 100. 4., 130. 3.
[5] IV. 2. 15., 3. 11., I. 71. 2, 3.
[6] X. 68. 2., III. 53. 7.; X. 62. 3.
[7] *jyéshṭham áñgirasām*, I. 127. 2.

the friend of the gods. The dawn, as also Soma, receives the epithet *áñgirastamā.*[1] The Virūpāḥ, the group of nine and the group of ten, different classes of Añgirases, are said to be born from the fire.[2] The group of nine are expressly identified with Agni's rays.[3] The fathers are the guardians of the sun, who give the light.[4] Through the confusion of the glance of the eye with a beam of light, they are represented as looking upon the earth, upon the creation of the world, and even reflexively upon Agni;[5] they are the spies of Mitra and Varuṇa.[6] Their participation in the creation and ordering of the world is based on their association with the different forms of Agni. "They measured with devising calculation the pair of twins (heaven and earth) of common origin and a common home, they weave again and again a new web in the sky, in the (aërial) ocean, the wise and brilliant ones." "The Añgirases made the sun to rise and spread out the earth."[7] Their place in the building metaphor is especially connected with Agni of the sacrifice; their preparing a place for him, their father, is parallel to the act of supporting the heaven. "They prepared an abode

[1] IX. 107. 6.; VII. 75. 1., 79. 3.
[2] *dáçagve saptásye*, IV. 51. 4.; X. 62. 5, 6.
[3] VI. 6. 3.
[4] X. 107. 1., 154. 5., I. 115. 2.
[5] I. 164. 4., X. 177. 1, 2., I. 185. 1.
[6] VII. 87. 3., cf. IX. 73. 7.
[7] I. 159. 4., X. 62. 3., cf. V. 44. 6.

for their father, they provided him skilfully with a large and glorious abode; they supported their parents (heaven and earth) apart with a support; sitting down (in the sacrifice) they placed him there (as a pillar) upright and powerful."[1]

Again, through the identification of the fathers with the light, they are brought into connection with the metaphor of generation. It was through Agni that their ancestors were enabled to give birth to their successors.[2] The fathers are united with the Dawn, and desire with her to beget male children.[3] In a hymn to Soma they are mentioned along with the morning sun as having placed the germ in the earth;[4] and the fruitfulness of heaven and earth, which give birth to gods and men, is described as produced by the fathers.[5]

The mystical union of the fathers with the rays of light is the fundamental idea underlying the abstruse allusions of the two hymns which will next occupy our attention. In the first hymn (X. 56.), which is a funeral hymn, the poet bids the deceased man unite himself with the beams of the heavenly light; he takes occasion to celebrate the power and greatness of the fathers, to whom the spirit

[1] III. 31. 12., cf. X. 92. 15. That the abode is the place of sacrifice is proved by verse 9.

[2] I. 68. 8, 9.

[3] IV. 2. 15., X. 61. 10, 11., cf. VI. 44. 23.

[4] IX. 83. 3., cf. I. 164. 36.

[5] X. 64. 14.

of the departed is journeying; and ends with a statement of the success of the journey for which he has prayed.

1. "One light hast thou here, and yonder another, unite thyself with the third (and highest);[1] uniting thyself with a body mayest thou be welcome and dear to the gods in the birth place on high.

2. May that body of thine, thou strong horse,[2] bearing thy body provide us with good things, and thee with protection; mayest thou without swerving establish the great gods here for a support as thine own light in the sky.

3. Thou art strong as a horse;[2] by this thy strength mayest thou go to the yearning maidens,[3] on an easy path to the (land of) praise, and to the sky, according to the first and true ordinances, on an easy path to the gods with an easy flight.

4. Of their greatness the fathers also have obtained a portion; the gods have placed insight in them as gods;[4] and they have embraced in themselves all

[1] The same idea finds expression in X. 16. 5., X. 14. 8. The third light is the light in the highest region; the reckoning naturally begins from the place where the speaker stands, cf. IX. 86. 27., X. 1. 3., 123. 8. Similarly Vishṇu's third step upwards is the step which lands him in the highest region.

[2] Ludwig takes *vājin* as the man's name.

[3] A metaphorical interpretation is most consonant with the context; hence probably they are the waters of the sky or the dawns.

[4] For this bold application of the name *devá* to the sacrificers, compare III. 7. 7., 54. 17., IV. 2. 17., VIII. 48. 3., X. 53. 4., and see Zimmer, Altindisches Leben, p. 205.

energies;[1] these (go forth and) enter again into their bodies.[2]

5. With power they strode through the whole region of the air, measuring the unmeasured ancient stations; in their bodies they enclosed all existing things; they produced[3] in many forms offspring from themselves in continued succession.

6. Here and on high[4] as sons they brought and set up the Asura-god, who bringeth light (Agni in the sacrifice below and above); by their third action as fathers they have placed their own offspring, the power of fathers, upon the earth, a thread spun out continuously.[5]

7. As in a ship over a flood hath Bṛihadukta with blessings mightily translated his offspring, over the regions of the air, over all the impassable ways, placing them in the heavenly as in the earthly regions."

The interpretation of one or two expressions in the hymn is uncertain; the general sense is clear. The rays of light are here the bodies of the fathers, which emanate from the sun, assume the forms of all things on the earth and of the later sacrificers, the descendants of the fathers, and again return to

[1] The meaning assigned to *átvishuḥ* in this passage in the Pet. Lex. is 'excite, call into life;' *tvishé* in VII. 82. 6. is translated 'to cause to arise.'

[2] Compare I. 72. 5, 9.

[3] *lit.* they caused to stream forth from themselves in succession.

[4] *lit.* in two ways.

[5] Compare A. V. X. 2. 17.

their birth-place in the sky from which they had extended themselves.

In the next hymn we have the same general conception of the mystical action of the fathers; but it is the poet himself who desires to attain in spirit the position of the ancient sacrificers. This peculiar form of thought, frequently recurring in the later literature, by which the aspirant identifies himself with the object of his aspiration, is exemplified in two ways in the Ṛigveda. Either the poets describe the ecstasy caused by the performance of the sacrifice and the singing of hymns, or perhaps more exactly by the intoxicating draughts of soma-juice, as a state of divine blessedness; or they anticipate the glories of the heavenly world which appear to them in visions of light. "We have drunk soma, we are become immortal; we have reached the light, we have found the gods." "And now that I have attained the sight of Varuṇa, his face seemeth to me as the face of Agni; the light that shineth in heaven and the darkness may he, the ruler, bring me thither to behold their form."[1] The same idea occurs in a late hymn (X. 136.), which describes the free course of the ascete (*múni*) through the air

[1] VIII. 48. 3, 11., VII. 88. 2-4.; cf. I. 125. 5., X. 31. 3., V. 30. 1, 2., VI. 9. 6., X. 2. 3., VIII. 78. 1., X. 130. 6., I. 25. 18. Ordinary knowledge is obtained *purushatvátā* V. 48. 5. Such passages may contain the original form of the later conception of inspiration that the hymns were seen by the Ṛishis.

as a spirit, and contains a further resemblance with our hymn in representing the *múni* as walking on the road of the Gandharvas, whereas in all other passages (except IX. 113. 3.) the Ṛigveda recognizes one Gandharva only.

III. 38. 1. "I will meditate a hymn as a carpenter, galloping as a fast horse at a strong pole; striving towards[1] the heavenly desirable regions, I long to behold the wise with insight.

2. Seek then the mighty generations of the wise; they by steadfastness and well-doing procured an abode in the sky; these are thy profitable guidances;[2] they whom the mind desires are now come to the firmament of heaven.

3. There they assume[3] hidden forms, and anoint heaven and earth to rule over them; measuring them with measuring-rods, and making them fast and broad, they set the great worlds apart, firmly fixed for security.[4]

4. They all adorn the rising (sun); clothed in splendour he moveth with his own brilliance; that is the mighty form of the Asura-bull; he who

[1] In the translation of *abhí mármṛiçat* I have followed the Pet. Lex. The form occurs here only in the Ṛigveda; but compare *abhí mṛiçe* I. 145. 4., II. 10. 5.; *prābhi mármṛiçat* I. 140. 5.

[2] For the form of expression compare X. 32. 7.

[3] Grassmann in his translation neglects the Ātm. p., cf. X. 5. 2., III. 1. 8., I. 6. 4.

[4] The translation of *dhā́yase* 'is obscure,' Pet. Lex. Ludwig renders 'zur Nahrung,' Grassmann 'zur Labung.'

possesseth all forms (*viçvárūpa*) cometh to the waters of ambrosia.[1]

5. The first, the more excellent bull[2] is born, these are his manifold invigorating draughts. Ye two sons of heaven[3] (or of Dyaus) through the hymns of the sacrifice possess the sovereignty, ye two kings, from of old.

6. Ye adorn in the sacrificial assembly, ye two kings, the three worlds, all the dwelling-places;[4] I saw there, coming thither in the spirit (*mánasā*), the Gandharvas in their course, whose hair traileth in (or as) the wind.[5]

7. That companionship[6] of the cow (dawn) with the forms of the strong bull they establish here; clothing themselves in one and another Asura-form the cunning artists determine his shape.

8. That golden light, which Savitar hath here

[1] The Pet. Lex. translates 'the forces of eternity;' a somewhat similar passage is I. 35. 6., compare also X. 139. 6.

[2] The sun, cf. V. 44. 8.

[3] Of the two kings one will almost certainly be Varuṇa; the other may be Mitra, or Indra, or Soma cf. IX. 95. 4., VI. 75. 18., or more probably Yama cf. X. 14. 7., 97. 16., 123. 6.

[4] 'The many places of sacrifice,' according to Ludwig's explanation; he quotes V. S. 23. 49., "I ask of thee to learn it, O friend of the gods, if thou art arrived thither in spirit (*mánasā*) where Vishṇu receives sacrifice at his three steps on which all the world is set."

[5] cf. VIII. 7. 8., III. 14. 3.

"But here there is no light
Save what from heaven is with the breezes blown."
—Keats, Ode to a Nightingale.

[6] This is the meaning for *sákmya* suggested in the Pet. Lex.

shed forth, none shall keep from me;[1] he covereth the spreading worlds with praise as a young woman covereth her offspring.

9. In the form of that divine blessedness which ye have established in the great and ancient one, may ye two embrace us;[2] all the Virūpāḥ, the cunning artists, behold the works of him who standeth protecting (the world) with his tongue (fire)."

The description of the cosmological importance of the sacrifice would, however, be incomplete without a reference to the prayer or hymn of sacrifice, the regulated utterance of the sacrificial priests. The prayer is mentioned especially as the instrument through which the Ṛishis effect their works and obtain children.[3] It is coupled with the fire, soma, and ghee as their bride; and thus adds one more element of complication to the interpretation of the different cows and nurses of Agni. But it is also mentioned once or twice alone as a power influencing the course of nature. "Adoration (*námas*) hath supported the heaven and the earth."[4] The place

[1] Ludwig translates, "that is the light of this Savitar, not mine." If with Grassmann we treat the clause as elliptical, we must supply some sense of frequent occurrence with *nákir*; for such a sense compare I. 69. 7., VI. 30. 2., VI. 7. 5., IV. 30. 23., VII. 32. 5., VIII. 28. 4., X. 132. 3., I. 155. 5. The general meaning will be that of the Gāyatrī III. 62. 10.

[2] *lit.* what of the ancient ye have established of the great, divine blessedness, be ye around us.

[3] *prajā́vatā vácasā*, I. 76. 4.: V. 45. 11. etc.

[4] VI. 51. 8.

of Vāc and Vācaspati in the cosmogonic system will be dealt with later. In II. 24, 5–7. the sacrifices, old and new, are personified as *kaváyaḥ*, and represented as discovering the devices of the Paṇayaḥ against the laws of nature, and bringing back the hidden fire.[1]

So far we have been considering the power of the earthly sacrifice in causing the great works of nature, and in elevating the worshippers to a position of friendship and almost of equality with the gods. The peculiar analogical or typical logic of the Ṛigveda receives, however, more striking illustration from the heavenly sacrifice. The whole ritual of sacrifice with all its appurtenances, its priests and offerings, were bodily translated from the sphere of human action to the world of the gods. The gods become the rich patrons for whom the sacrifice is performed, the *yájamānāḥ* ; Agni, the mediator between earth and heaven, becomes their priest; he is established by the gods in his priestly office, as the typical sacrificer.[2] "First the gods produced the hymn of praise, then Agni, then the offering, so Agni became their sacrifice."[3] He is the *puróhita*, the appointed priest, of the gods, or perhaps, in the classical sense, their family priest. The gods are even said to have obtained immortality through the

[1] cf. III. 4. 5.

[2] VIII. 23. 18.

[3] X. 88. 8.

sacrifice by drinking the soma, or as the gift of Agni or of Bṛihaspati, who therefore receives the title 'father of all the gods.'[1] In X. 53. 10. it would seem that it was the soma made by the Ṛibhus through which the gods obtained immortality. Heaven and earth, the primeval father and mother, are, in particular, the first sacrificers, whose priest is Agni, their first-born, the sun or the lightning.[2]

The cosmological significance of the divine sacrifice finds particular expression in three hymns of the tenth book. Two of these (81 and 82) are addressed to a god Viçvakarman, who combines in his person the characters of a primeval divine sacrificer and of a creator. We have already seen these two functions united in Agni. We have further seen how the sun, or an abstraction derived from the sun, under the names of Hiraṇyagarbha and Aja, figures as at once the germ and the creator of the universe; the sacrificial side of Agni's character, as the primeval priest or father, and in this sense the creator of the world, is embodied in the person of Viçvakarman, who is thus a parallel figure to Hiraṇyagarbha, with many common characteristics, and who was in the later literature identified with him. The name

1. In many passages the word *devá* may refer primarily to the deified ancient sacrificers. The Maruts, however, are particularly represented as sacrificers, III. 32. 2., V. 29, 3, 6., X. 122. 5.; and probably this is the meaning of their attribute *vedhás*.

2. IV. 56. 2., II. 2. 3.

Viçvakarman occurs twice more only in the Ṛigveda, both times beside *viçvádeva.* "Thou, Indra, art over all; thou hast made the sun to shine, thou art the all-worker (*viçvákarman*), the all-god, the mighty one."[1] In the other passage it is an epithet of the sun, "by whom all existing things are brought to light, the all-worker, possessed of universal godhead."[2] A third passage, in which the form *viçvákarma* occurs, is ambiguous. The hymn seems to be placed in the mouth of Vācaspati *sapatnahán,* 'the lord of speech, slayer of rivals.'[3] The mention of Vācaspati would seem to point a reference to verse 7 of our first hymn; but the hymn is rather to be compared with the incantations of the Atharvaveda, in which less regard is paid to the deity invoked, than to the form of invocation.

X. 81. 1.[4] "He who, sacrificing all existing things, as Ṛishi, as sacrificer, sat down (for sacrifice) our father; he desiring treasure[5] by prayer entered, the first worshipper, among men on earth.[6]

2. What was his standing-place? what was the

[1] VIII. 98. 2.

[2] X. 170. 4.

[3] X. 166. 4. For another interpretation of this hymn see Zimmer, Altindisches Leben, p. 175.

[4] Some verses of these hymns have been translated by Professor F. Max Müller in his Hibbert Lectures, p. 293 f.

[5] cf. X. 45. 11., 46. 2. The only similar form to *prathamachdd* is *kavichdd,* an epithet of Indra and Agni III. 12. 3.; the translation remains doubtful.

[6] cf. II. 34. 11.

support? how was it?[1] whence Viçvakarman produced the earth, and revealed the sky by his power, the all-seer.

3. He who hath on all sides an eye, on all sides a mouth, on all sides an arm, and on all sides a foot, producing heaven and earth, weldeth them together with his arms as wings (*i.e.* fanning the flame, cf. X. 72. 2.), the sole god.

4. What indeed was the wood? what too was that tree, from which they fashioned the heaven and the earth? Seek, ye thoughtful men, by your thought, that on which he took his stand when he made all things fast.

5. The highest, the lowest, and the middle sacrificial stations, that are thine, O Viçvakarman, and also those here, teach to thy companions at the sacrifice, thou blessed one; do thou sacrifice to thyself[2] delighting thyself.

6. O Viçvakarman, do thou, delighting in the offering, thyself sacrifice to heaven and earth. May other men about us be fools; let us have a beneficent lord.

7. We invoke Viçvakarman, the lord of speech

[1] The first pāda is too short by three syllables, or the second by four; the employment of *katamát* 'which,' not 'what,' referring to one of a known class, may point to a corruption of the text. Verses 3, 4, 5, and 7 have each an extra syllable.

[2] The expression may be translated with Ludwig and Grassmann "sacrifice thine own body." Verse 6 and the comparison with X. 7. 6., VI. 11. 2. render the interpretation given above more probable.

(*vācáspáti*), who moveth at a thought, for help to-day in our arduous work (*i.e.* 'in the sacrifice,' as *havishi*, verse 5); may he hear all our invocations with favour, who bringeth all good for our welfare, whose workings are successful."[1]

X. 82. 1. "The father of the eye, wise in spirit, produced these two worlds, submerged in ghee; as soon as the eastern ends were made fast, heaven and earth extended themselves.

2. Viçvakarman, whose power is wide as his wisdom, was the ordainer and disposer, and the highest apparition; their (the fathers') offerings revel in rich juice, there where the one, they tell us, is above the seven Ṛishis.

3. Who is our father, the generator, the disposer, who knoweth the stations (in heaven and earth) and all existing things; who ordained the forms of the gods, even he alone; to him all other beings go for information (*i.e.* to learn their destination).

4. The ancient Ṛishis offered to him treasure in abundance as singers; who, settled in the earthly and heavenly regions,[2] prepared these things that have come into existence.

5. That which is before the heaven and before

[1] *Sādhúkarman.* The play on Viçvakarman's name is obvious. Probably in both words the reference is primarily to the special meaning of *kárman* 'sacrificial work.'

[2] Reading *nishattáḥ*. The Pet. Lex. derives *asúrte súrte* from the root *svar* 'shine,' cf. *atúrta, adṛishṭa*, K.Z. xxvii. p. 63.

the earth, before the Asura-gods (or the gods and the Asuras); what first germ did the waters receive, where all the gods appeared together?[1]

6. The waters received that first germ, where all the gods were collected; it rested on the navel of the Unborn that alone (*ékam*), in which all existing things abide.

7. Ye will not find him who gave birth to these things; another thing hath arisen among you; covered with darkness and stammering, wander the wanton singers of hymns."

In artistic composition and arrangement the two hymns are as weak as the hymn to Hiraṇyagarbha. If we eliminate the play on the word *viçva* and the general expressions of creation, the nearest analogy to the figure of Viçvakarman is Agni, whose sacrificial character is especially alluded to in the phrase *svayám yajasva tanvàm* "sacrifice to thine own self." The derivation of the conception from the sun is seen in the expressions 'the father of the eye,' 'the all-seer' (the latter an expression applied elsewhere twice to the sun and once to Soma), 'the highest apparition.'[2] Verses 5 and 6 of the second hymn find their parallel in verses 7 and 8 of the hymn to Hiraṇyagarbha. Aja, the Unborn, seems here to be identified with Viçvakarman. There can then be little doubt as to the motive of the two hymns. They are based on

[1] cf. III. 54. 9., V. 44. 6, 7., X. 61. 19.

[2] IV. 1. 6., 6. 6., for other references see Grassmann's Lexicon.

the conception, already described, of the sun as the first-born of the world and the prototype of subsequent generation, and contain little more than an adaptation of this conception (not necessarily of hymn X. 121) to a sacrificial god, an adaptation which may be ascribed to the special bias of the Ṛishis.

In connection with the sacrifice the title 'lord of speech' requires special examination. The title is also applied twice to Soma. Vāc, 'speech,' is celebrated alone in two whole hymns, X. 71. and X. 125.,[1] of which the former shows that the primary application of the name was to the voice of the hymn, the means of communication between heaven and earth at the sacrifice. The other hymn illustrates the constant assimilation of the varied phenomena of nature to the sacrifice; all that has a voice in nature, the thunder of the storm, the reawaking of life at dawn, with songs of rejoicing over the new birth of the world, are embodied in this Vāc in the same way as it is said of Bṛihaspati, that he embraces all things that are. It is thus another expression for that idea of the unity of the world, which we have seen crowning the mystical speculation of all the more abstract hymns of the collection. Again, as the natural phenomena corresponding to Hiraṇyagarbha and Viçvakarman are the phenomena

[1] The comparison of verses 2, 3, and 7 of this hymn with VIII. 100. 10, 11., I. 164. 34, 35, establishes the accuracy of the tradition which connects the hymn with Vāc.

of light; so also corresponding to Vāc we find, though in a very much less marked degree, the analogies of the breath of the wind, and of the flow of the voice, represented by the river Sarasvatī, hymns being frequently compared to streams.[1] The wind is the breath or life of the gods (*ātmán*), and the embryo of the world; with it the soul of man unites itself after death;[2] Vāyu is called the lord of the *ṛitá*.[3] Sarasvatī fills earth and air; she is continually coupled in invocation with the prayers;[4] and becomes later an impersonation of language. The last two verses of X. 125. will suffice as an illustration of the general terms in which the universality of the nature of Vāc finds expression. "I give birth to the father on the summit of the world, my birth-place is in the waters in the sea; thence I spread forth over all existing things, with the crown of my head I touch yonder Heaven. I too breathe a strong breath as the wind, supporting all existing things; beyond the heaven, beyond the earth, I have become so great by my power."

The hymns to Viçvakarman make no attempt to explain in what way the process of sacrifice could be regarded as an act of creation. We are told little more than that he was a primeval sacrificer

[1] V. 11. 5., I. 113. 18.

[2] X. 168. 4., X. 16. 3.

[3] VIII. 26. 21.

[4] VI. 61. 11.; X. 65. 13., VII. 35. 11., cf. I. 3. 12.

and also a creator; we have no hint how to combine the two ideas into a harmonious unity. The next hymn, the Purushasūkta, one of the very latest hymns of the Ṛigveda, is an attempt to solve this difficulty. The legend of the formation of the universe from the different parts of a giant is well known to comparative mythologists;[1] here we see how the Ṛishis adapted the myth to serve their own ends.

X. 90. 1. "The Man (*púrusha*) had a thousand heads, a thousand eyes, and a thousand feet; he covered the earth in all directions, and extended ten finger-breadths beyond.

2. The Man was all this that hath been and will be made, and a possessor of the immortality which groweth great by food (offered in sacrifice).

3. Such was his greatness; yea, the Man was still mightier; all that hath been made was one quarter of him, three quarters of him were the immortals in heaven.

4. With three quarters the Man mounted up, one quarter came here again; thence he strode out on all sides over that which eateth and that which eateth not.

5. From him the Virāj[2] was born, and from the

[1] cf. *e.g.* Orphic Hymn 26, page 202 in Abel's edition.

[2] Virāj, whose name in X. 159. 3. appears to mean 'queen,' would seem to be the female counterpart of Purusha, as Aditi of Daksha in X. 72. 4, 5.; cf. Bṛihadār. Up. 4. 2. 3., and Dr. Muir's note in his translation of this hymn, Original Sanskrit Texts, vol. v. p. 369.

Virāj the Man; as soon as he was born, he reached out over the earth eastwards and westwards.

6. When the gods prepared the sacrifice with the Man as the offering, the spring was the sacrificial butter, the summer was the fuel, and the autumn was the offering.

7. As a victim on the (sacrificial) grass they anointed the Man who was born in the beginning; him the gods sacrificed, the Sādhyas[1] and the Ṛishis.

8. When the sacrifice was completed, they collected the dripping fat from it; it formed the beasts of the air, of the wild places, and of the village.

9. When the sacrifice was completed, the Ṛig-hymns and the Sāma-hymns were born from it, the incantations were born, the Yajus was born from it.

10. From it were born the horses, all the cattle that have two rows of teeth; the kine were born from it; from it the goats and sheep were born.

11. When they disposed the Man, into how many parts did they form him?[2] What are his mouth, his arms, his thighs, and his feet called?

12. His mouth was the Brahman; his arms were made the Rājanya; his thighs were the Vaiçya; and the Çūdra was born from his feet.

[1] The Sādhyas would seem to be divine ancient sacrificers. Compare X. 109. 4.; also X. 191. 2., VII. 21. 7., and X. 130.

[2] Or elliptically, following Professor Avery's suggestion, Journal of the American Oriental Society, vol. xi. p. cxlix, "dividing him into all the parts into which they formed him."

13. The moon was born from his mind, the sun from his eye; Indra and Agni from his mouth, and Vāyu was born from his breath.

14. From his navel came the air; from his head arose the sky, from his feet the earth, from his ear the regions; so they formed the worlds.

15. He had seven enclosing logs of fuel, and thrice seven layers of fuel; when the gods performed the sacrifice, they bound the Man as victim.

16. (=I. 164. 50.) So the gods sacrificed a sacrifice sacrificially: they were the first sacrificial ordinances. Those mighty ones attained to heaven, where the ancient Sādhyas abide as gods."

We have now passed in review the three most circumstantial explanations of the origin of the world. In the first chapter it was regarded as a work of art; and since the principal manufacture known to the men of the time was the working of wood, the world was pronounced a production of builders and joiners. In the second chapter the origin of the world was ascribed to the agency of that visible process which is the cause of all natural, as opposed to mechanical, production. In the argument of this chapter the origin of the world was supposed to have been effected by a similar instrumentality to that which is represented as the most efficacious in the hands of man, the formal sacrifice. The three explanations are not mutually exclusive; any two of them or all three are frequently combined together in one verse. The classification adopted in this essay is, therefore, to be regarded as one of practical convenience only. Further, it must not be supposed that what is here described as the system of the Ṛishis was their exclusive possession. There may have been laymen whose views were more sacerdotal than those of the priests; as there may have been, and doubtless were, priests to whom speculation was dearer than ritual.[1] On the other hand, a classification based on later forms of thought would have been positively misleading. We may very easily persuade ourselves that in some isolated verse we have discovered the starting-point of a later philosophy, where the comparison of similar passages shows that it was only the poverty of our imagination which confined the meaning within our own particular range of thought. The Ṛigveda must be made its own commentary. It is a not infrequent occurrence that a whole complex of modern ideas finds its most happy and appropriate expression in an old term, or a proper name or attribute, or in the words of an ancient saying. The words themselves have contributed nothing to the formation of the ideas; they had lost their first meaning and were fast falling into oblivion, when the breath of a spirit from another sphere inspired them with a new vitality.

[1] cf. X. 71. 11.

CHAPTER IV.

THE ORDER OF THE WORLD.

ATTENTION has already been drawn to the narrow boundary-line which often separates the expression of the superficial guesses of unscientific thinkers from the expression of the profoundest results of modern philosophy and science. We meet continually in our hymns with forms of expression, appearing at first sight to be the vehicle of grand thought, placed side by side with puerile and foolish conceits. Some general rule is needed for the guidance of the interpreter. In the case of an individual man it may be an impossibility to draw a line of circumscription marking out the range of his thought; in the case, however, of a class of men, the difficulty will naturally be increased of defining the capacity of the deepest or acutest thinker among them; but we can draw inferences as to the construction which they as a class will put upon a given expression, and so reflexively as to the sense in which an author addressing them expects his words to be understood. The difficulties of the critic will be found to concentrate themselves for the most part on the interpretation of abstract words. Common experience teaches us that an unscientific speaker makes a large use of a limited number of abstract words in different senses, neglecting for the time being in each particular application of his terms the senses, which in other contexts he would himself intend by them. The terms are rich in the variety of their meanings, the connection of which with one another may not appear strictly logical; but the connotation of the terms in individual expressions is limited. The character of the hymns of the Ṛigveda is in general anything but philosophic or scientific; consequently, in order to find the motive for the use of particular words or phrases we are bound to seek on every occasion the most special meaning which the context will admit, at the same time remembering that no such need of a strict limitation was probably present to the mind of the author.

The word used to denote the conception of the order of the world is *ṛitá*.[1] Everything in the universe which is conceived as showing regularity of action may be said to have the *ṛitá* for its principle. In its most general application the conception expressed by the word occupied to some extent the place of natural and moral law, fate, or

[1] The account which Professor F. Max Müller has given of this world in his Hibbert Lectures, pp. 237 ff., is based on his view of the etymology.

the will of a supreme god. It is the great and mighty *ṛitá*,[1] which gods and men obey, and beside which the Vedic gods sink into the position of angels or heavenly spirits. The *ṛitá* was, however, in itself too stationary, too conservative, and purely regulative to be endowed with the individual life necessary to a god; it remained an abstract idea and was not an object of direct adoration.

More usually the meaning of the word as applied to the natural world connects itself with the alternation of day and night, the regular passage of the sun through the heavens, or the unswerving motion of the rain in its fall from heaven and of the streams along their courses. This last application of the word may have determined its special sense of 'water' in the later language. The limited meaning as applied to the regular celestial phenomena is illustrated by the phrase, 'the place of the *ṛitá*,' used specifically for the sky. "The Maruts come from afar from the seat of the *ṛitá*."[2] Vishṇu is the embryo of the *ṛitá*.[3] This sense is perhaps also the ground of the association of the word *ṛitá* with the metaphorical antithesis of light and darkness, the types of happi-

[1] *mahát*, *bṛihát*, cf. *bṛihát svàr*—

> "He might not:—no, though a primeval god:
> The sacred seasons might not be disturbed."
>
> Keats, Hyperion.

[2] *parāvátaḥ sádanād ṛitásya* IV. 21. 3.

[3] I. 156. 3.

ness and distress, and of moral right and wrong. The word is used interchangeably with *satyá* 'reality, truth,' and hence 'light,' 'belonging to the light;' *ánṛita* is the most usual antithesis to *satyá*.[1] The sun figures in connection with both terms; "the earth is supported by truth, the sky is supported by the sun, the Ādityas exist by the *ṛitá*." "The flowing of the streams is *ṛitá*, the expansion of the sun's light is truth." The sun is "the true light set on the sure support of the sky."[2] To the Ṛishi, however, the type of regularity on earth was the sacrifice; the word is therefore specially employed in the sense of sacrifice. Agni is said to sacrifice the *ṛitá*.[3] The *ṛitá* has its chariot, its ship, its horses, bulls, cows, and the like, in all which cases the reference is primarily or exclusively to the sacrifice. The seat of the *ṛitá* becomes the place of sacrifice.

We proceed to the discussion of the place of the *ṛitá* in cosmogony. The discussion limits itself naturally to those passages where *ṛitá* is employed in its cosmic sense, putting on one side such expressions as 'offspring' or 'embryo of the *ṛitá*' applied to Agni and Soma, because fire and soma-juice were produced at the sacrifice. The principle of the order of the world, of the regularity of cosmic

[1] VII. 56. 12., IX. 113. 4., III. 6. 10.; IV. 5. 5., VIII. 62. 12., VII. 49. 3. cf. V. 12. 4., Bṛihadār. Up. 1. 4. 14.

[2] X. 85. 1., I. 105. 12., X. 170. 2.

[3] I. 75. 5.

phenomena, was conceived by the Ṛishis to have existed as a principle before the manifestation of any phenomena. The argument would seem to be somewhat as follows. The phenomena of the world are shifting and changeable, but the principle regulating the periodical recurrence of phenomena is constant; fresh phenomena are continually reproduced, but the principle of order remains the same; the principle, therefore, existed already when the earliest phenomena appeared; in the Vedic idiom it is their father, it has given birth to them. This parentage is exactly parallel to that of heaven and earth. Heaven and earth are the first according to or by reason of the *ṛitá*;[1] the gods are born of *ṛitá*. The view that the principle must precede the manifestation appears to be the motive of the following short and rather incomprehensible hymn, probably one of the latest in the collection.[2]

X. 190. 1. "Order (*ṛitá*) and truth were born from kindled heat, the night was born, then the watery flood.

2. From the watery flood the year was born, disposing day and night, the ruler of all that closeth the eye.

3. The Ordainer (*dhātár*) formed sun and moon in order, and heaven and earth, the regions of the air and the light."

[1] X. 12. 1.

[2] Since it is not divided up in the pada recension.

It will be observed that the year, day, and night come into existence before the sun, moon, heaven, and earth. The hymn is unique in its enumeration of progressive stages in the growth of the world. In no other hymn is the origin of the world viewed as a gradual process. Account must, however, be taken of the necessities of the style in which the hymns are composed, admitting of fragmentary allusions of every kind, but not of the full treatment at one time of any one thought. In one passage at the beginning of the well-known physician's hymn, we read that "the plants came into being three ages before the gods."[1] If the passage has any cosmological significance, and from the context this appears very improbable, it is still too isolated in the Ṛigveda to form the basis of an argument.

The expression 'born from the *ṛitá*'[2] is indistinguishable from the equally common phrases 'born in the *ṛitá*' or 'according to the *ṛitá*,' or the more indefinite expressions 'born of the *ṛitá*,' 'embryo of the *ṛitá*,' *ṛitajā́*, *ṛitejā́*, *ṛitáprajāta*, *ṛitájāta*, the last of which is analysed in one passage (VI. 7. 1.) into *ṛité jātá*. The separate manifestations of the *ṛitá* are expressed by the plural *ṛitā́ni*, where each phenomenon is itself regarded as a *ṛitá*. Thus the

[1] *triyugám* X. 97. 1.

[2] In II. 13. 1. *ṛitú*, the mother, is probably the time of sacrifice. In the Atharvaveda, xix. 53 and 54, it is time in general, *kālá*, that appears as the parent of all things.

gods are the protectors or leaders of *ṛitá*; the dawn directs the reins of *ṛitá*; the dawns or the sun produce *ṛitá*. Or again, the causes of these manifestations may be regarded as the causes of the principle, and so we return to the familiar paradox that the sons begat their parent. Heaven and earth, morning and night, are the mothers of the *ṛitá*.

The best illustration of the ideas connected with the order of the world will be an examination of the character of Varuṇa, the chief of the lords of natural order. Varuṇa is in the Ṛigveda primarily the great king over all, whose throne is in the sky, the god of peaceful dominion as opposed to the warrior Indra.[1] From his throne on high he looks down upon all that happens in the world, and into the heart of man. "He knoweth the path of the birds, that fly through the air; he knoweth the ships as lord of the sea; he knoweth the way of the spreading, high, and mighty wind; and he knoweth those who dwell above it. He beholdeth with insight that which is hidden, that which is done and yet to be done."[2] As king he ordains all that happens on the earth, and as legislator he

[1] VII. 82. 5. A full description of Varuṇa's character, together with a discussion of the origin and development of the conception of the god, will be found in Professor A. Hillebrandt's Mitra and Varuṇa, Breslau, 1877.

[2] I. 25. 7, 9, 11.

lays down the laws. The Maruts receive their impulse from Indra, but their instructions from Varuṇa.[1] His activity shows itself pre-eminently in the control of the most regular phenomena of nature, the course of the sun, and of the rivers. Mitra and Varuṇa set the sun in heaven as a shining chariot. "King Varuṇa made a path for the sun for it to follow," and a path for the streams.[2] The seven rivers of the sky, as the seven rivers of the earth, are under his control. In I. 24. verse 10. the poet wonders whither the stars go in the daytime, and his explanation is that "Varuṇa's laws are inviolable; the moon wanders shining through the night." Mitra and Varuṇa have ordained the succession of years, months, and days.[3] And Varuṇa's power is not limited to the natural world; as judge he administers his own moral code, and is especially invoked for forgiveness of sins against fellow-men. Indra is mentioned as the soldier who punishes offenders against Varuṇa's laws.[4]

These laws are in Vedic language *vratā́ni*; the nearest English translation of the word is perhaps 'courses of action' or 'ways of life.'[5] It is used

[1] X. 66. 2.

[2] V. 63. 7., I. 24. 8., VII. 60. 4., 63. 5., 87. 1., II. 28. 4.

[3] VII. 66. 11., I. 25. 8.

[4] X. 113. 5.

[5] For the etymology of the word *vratá* see a note by Professor Whitney in the Journal of the American Oriental Society, vol. xi. p. ccxxix. 'Course of action, behaviour,' is the meaning he assigns to it.

especially with verbs of motion or of following, in one place with the addition of the words 'as it were with the feet,'[1] and with the prepositions *ánu* 'after,' and its converse *áti*; in these constructions *vratá* alone is equivalent to *ṛitásya pánthāḥ*, the path of the *ṛitá*. It is used of the characteristic occupations of gods and of men.[2] A good wife is a wife who follows the *vratá* of her husband. The *vratā́ni* of a superior power are said to overcome those of an inferior; the *vratā́ni* of the other gods yield to Indra; he places himself above all other *vratā́ni*; he conquers the *vratā́ni* of the great flood.[3] All things are said to be in the *vratá* of a powerful god.[4] Thus the meaning of the word takes its colour from the person to whom it is applied: a description of the *vratā́ni* of Varuṇa is a description of his activity.

The *vratā́ni* of Varuṇa are his royal ordinances. Soma is twice compared to a king whose *vratā́ni* are good;[5] and the ordinances of king Soma are praised as the *vratā́ni* of Mitra and Varuṇa.[6] The criterion of excellence in a good lawgiver and judge is the firmness and impartiality of his decisions. What he has once determined must remain as a

[1] V. 67. 3.
[2] IX. 112. 1., X. 37. 5.
[3] VI. 14. 3., III. 60. 6., VIII. 32. 28., X. 111. 4.
[4] Indra III. 30. 4.; Parjanya V. 83. 5.
[5] IX. 20. 5., 57. 3.
[6] I. 91. 3. = IX. 88. 8.

rule to bind all subsequent decisions. Hence we are continually told of Varuṇa that his *vratắni* stand fast, are unalterable (*dhṛitávrata*). "For on thee, O thou that none may deceive, rest the immovable *vratắni* as on a mountain." They are the fixed ordinances according to which the sun travels through heaven, the streams flow into the ocean, and the actions of men are ruled.[1] The other gods follow the *vratắni* of Mitra and Varuṇa, they are in their *vratá*; poets pray that they may walk in Varuṇa's *vratá*;[2] and Mitra and Varuṇa follow the *vratá*, which they themselves have made, as a just king follows his own precedents.[3]

Thus Varuṇa occupies a position corresponding as nearly as possible to that of the *ṛitá*, of which he may almost be considered the personification. His *vratắni* are the *vratắni* of the *ṛitá*; the *ṛitá* is itself called the *ṛitá* of Mitra and Varuṇa; it is the principle of their activity, according to which they rule; they are the guides and protectors of the *ṛitá*; and Varuṇa punishes offenders against the *ṛitá*.[4] This sketch suffices to show how Varuṇa, the maintainer and ordainer of all that is constant in the world,

[1] II. 28. 8., cf. X. 65. 8.; VIII. 41. 1., I. 24. 10., X. 12. 5., "The king's heart is in the hand of the Lord as the watercourses: he turneth it whithersoever he will."—Prov. xxi. 1.

[2] VIII. 41. 7., X. 36. 13., I. 24. 15., II. 28. 2., VII. 87. 7.

[3] IV. 13. 2., V. 67. 3.

[4] III. 4. 7., II. 28. 4., X. 85. 1., V. 63. 7., II. 27. 8., VII. 40. 4., VII. 84. 4., cf. VII. 83. 9.

could be considered as the creator of the world. He differs from the deities mentioned in Chapter II in that he is in no way a productive agent in nature, his creative function is an inference from his presidential capacity; he differs from the *ṛitá* in that he is an agent and not a mere regulating principle. The following is one of the clearest hymns in which Varuṇa appears in this general character of the orderer, maintainer, and therefore creator of the world.

V. 85. 1. "I will sing forth a mighty and loud hymn to the king of all, acceptable to renowned Varuṇa; who hath struck out the earth, as a slayer of victims, a skin to spread forth before the sun.

2. He hath woven the air in the trees;[1] he hath placed speed in horses, and milk in kine; Varuṇa hath placed understanding in hearts, fire in water, the sun in the sky, and soma on the mountain.

3. Varuṇa poureth forth the cask, mouth downwards, over heaven, earth, and air, wherewith the king of all the world wetteth the land, as rain a corn-field.

4. Varuṇa wetteth the land, earth and sky, what time he wisheth to draw milk; the mountains clothe themselves in cloud; the tempestuous warriors[2] are let loose.

[1] Pet. Lex. 'clouds.'

[2] Maruts, V. 63. 4, 6., IV. 54. 5.

5. This great design of the renowned Asura, of Varuṇa will I proclaim — that, standing in the region of the air, he measureth out the earth with the sun as with a measuring-rod.

6. This great design of the most wise god hath none assailed, that the swift streaming rivers fill not the one sea with water.

7. What wrong we have ever done, O Varuṇa, to comrade or friend (with a play on the names Mitra and Aryaman), to companion or brother, to one of our own tribe or to stranger, loose it from us.

8. If we have cheated at play as dishonest players, be our sin real or such as we know not (*i.e.* imposed by a curse), cast all from us, O god, as loose bonds, and let us be thine own, O Varuṇa."[1]

The word translated 'design' (*māyá*) in verses 5 and 6 calls for special comment. It is apparently derived from an obsolete root *mā* (= *man*), 'to think,' and is used in the sense of planning a work of art, or a malicious attack on an enemy. It was, however, by the Ṛishis approximated to the existing root *mā* (*mi*), 'measure,'[2] and is thus applied to the

[1] The comparison with the Old Testament cannot fail to suggest itself. For such a comparison there is no more instructive chapter than Job, xxxviii.; there is scarcely a metaphor in that chapter which does not find its exact parallel in the Vedic descriptions of Varuṇa. The tone is, however, very different. The Hebrew poet is illustrating in detail the incomprehensible power of Jehovah, contrasted with the frailty of man.

[2] IX. 83. 3., cf. II. 17. 5., I. 159. 4., III. 38. 7.; see the article 'La māyā et le pouvoir créateur des divinités védiques' by M. Regnaud, in the Revue de l'histoire des religions, vol. xii. pp. 237 ff.

measuring skill of Mitra and Varuṇa in laying the foundations of the earth, and in directing the course of the sun and the waters. The original meaning of the word, denoting the artistic designing or planning of a work with the mental calculation of an architect, rather than the manual skill of a builder or carpenter, will explain how it is that it is only once applied to Tvashṭar,[1] and only once to the Ṛibhus.[2] The sun goes to his work knowing the design of the gods.[3] In V. 63. 7. the *māyá* of the Asura is placed side by side with the *dhárman* of Mitra and Varuṇa. This *māyá* of the Asura, Dyaus pitar, whose worship was practically a thing of the past at the time when our hymns were composed,[4] is mentioned elsewhere only in the instrumental case; Mitra and Varuṇa send rain according to, or by means of the design of the Asura; [5] the sun is anointed (with light) according to the design of the Asura. The *māyá* of the Asura is in other passages simply transferred to Varuṇa; the sun is called the *māyá* of Mitra and Varuṇa; or the name of the god is omitted and we are told that the sun shines *māyáyā* "according to design"[6] "These two children (sun and moon) wander one

[1] X. 53. 9.

[2] III. 60. 1. parallel to *çácī, dhī́, mánas.*

[3] X. 88. 6.

[4] Compare Dr. Bradke's Dyaus Asura, Halle, 1885.

[5] V. 63. 3.

[6] VIII. 41. 3.; III. 61. 7., cf. V. 63. 4.; I. 160. 3.

after the other according to design, they go dancing round the place of sacrifice; the one beholds all existing things, the other ordaining the times of the sacrifice is born again and again."[1] The English word 'design,' contrasted with the plural 'designs,' illustrates at the same time the malevolent sense of the plural of the Vedic word, a sense associated with the singular in one or two passages only.

The contemplation of this august god Varuṇa, who at first sight would appear worthy of exclusive adoration, recalls us, finally, to the consideration of the extent of the advance towards monotheism testified by our hymns. There are only two ways conceivable by which a religion can rise from a polytheistic to a monotheistic stage. Either one of the polytheistic gods can be elevated to a position of unique supremacy over all the others; or a new god can be introduced who shall supplant the old gods and reduce them to the condition of inferior spirits, demons, or non-entities. The elevation of an indigenous god may be caused by the influence of an external religious system, or in the absence of direct foreign influence may result from the gradual development of the religion through the action of philosophic thought or national enthusiasm working upon the religion, or through systematization of existing religious conceptions. That the impulse

[1] X. 85. 18.

towards monotheism was not the outcome of the religion of the priests, as presented to us in the Ṛigveda, will be shewn by an examination of the shortcomings of the two principal gods of the Ṛigveda, Indra and Varuṇa.

Varuṇa was compromised by his position of equality with Mitra, and his association with the other gods classed as Ādityas. Essentially a god of peace, he could not be invoked in the struggles for victory over hostile tribes, that blessing which lay nearest to the hearts of the kings who were the chief patrons of the sacrifice; as a stern god of justice he offered little attraction to the common people; his throne was set in heaven, and thus he had a limited, almost local, existence which offended the metaphysical sense of the philosophers. Very soon after the period of the composition of our hymns he was reduced from his exalted position to that of the god of the midnight sky, or of the waters.

The favourite god of the Ṛigveda is Indra. He is endowed with the functions and attributes of most of the other gods of the pantheon, including those of Varuṇa.[1] He is set free from the limitations of space and time. The whole universe cannot contain

[1] I. 101. 3. The following list contains passages in which actions characteristic of Varuṇa are ascribed to Indra: VIII. 40. 8., II. 24. 12., VII. 47. 3., X. 111. 3, 8., VIII. 37. 3., VII. 98. 6., V. 40. 8., X. 138. 6., cf. VII. 66. 11., I. 25. 8. Compare also M. Bergaigne's interpretation of IV. 42., La Religion védique, vol. iii. p. 143.

him; if there were a hundred heavens, and a hundred earths, and a thousand suns, they would not equal him;[1] he embraces all nations as a felloe the spokes of a wheel; he holds the two worlds in his fist; the earth and all creatures are as a grain of dust in his sight.[2] His dominion is not limited to past and present, it extends over all time. He is above all that has been, and that is to be born; in him are all heroïc deeds that have been done and will be done.[3] The conception of Indra was, however, too much hampered by association with popular legends, and his character too pronounced as that of a warrior, to be acceptable to the Brahmans; the unusual distinctness of his personality was incompatible with absolute supremacy. He remained a great god, the first of the Devas, but never became the highest deity.

The verses of our hymns which refer to an unique supreme being are not to be explained as products of the natural development of Vedic religion as represented to us by the Ṛishis. They are stray lights from an entirely different order of thought, which is represented later in the Upanishads. Tradition points unmistakeably to the inference that

[1] VIII. 70. 5. *Atha imā atistutaya ity ācakshate 'pi vā sampratyaya eva syād mahābhāgyād devatāyāḥ.* Nirukta 13. 1. Similar passages are I. 100. 15., 173. 6., VI. 30. 1.

[2] III. 30. 5., I. 63. 1., X. 119. 6.

[3] VIII. 89. 6., VIII. 63. 6.

the speculations which these latter contain were particularly characteristic of the royal class.[1] If we consider further that in the Vedic age the priests had not yet attained to the high position of sole authoritative teachers among the people which they afterwards arrogated to themselves, it will not perhaps be an improbable conjecture that the lay philosophy to which these verses bear witness was in its origin the production of members of princely families independent of the narrow system of the Ṛishis. Their introduction into the Ṛigveda shows that the compilers of that collection were not conscious of any incongruity, and may be taken as a sign that the ideas which they contain were the property of the few. The Ṛishis, for their part, were already inclined to regard the sacrifice as of more importance than the character of the gods to whom it was offered. The same indifference which is seen in the indefinite-

[1] "We may hope in course of time, in view of the wealth of material extant in the Ṛigveda, Atharvaveda, and the Brāhmaṇas, to be able to trace step by step how the sparks of philosophic light struck in the Ṛigveda glimmered brighter and brighter, till at last in the Upanishads they burst into that clear flame, which even now has power to enlighten and warm us. A number of tokens indicate that the real cherisher of these thoughts was originally the caste of the Kshatriyas rather than the caste of the priests, which was sated with ceremonial observances: over and over again in the Upanishads we come across the situation that the Brahman asks the Kshatriya for information, which the latter after various reflections on the impropriety of the proceeding imparts to him (cf. Bṛih. 2. 1., Kaush. 4. 1., Bṛih. 6. 2., Chānd. 5. 3., 5. 11., Kaush. 1. 1.)."—Deussen, Das System des Vedānta, p. 18.

ness of their conceptions of individual gods explains to some extent the fact that they had not energy enough to develope their theology into a monotheism. Their religion remained essentially polytheistic;[1] but side by side with the religion, independent of it, though not in hostility with it, there was a germ of mystic philosophy cherished by a few speculative thinkers, who recognized one supreme cause and bowed down in devotion before it.

[1] Compare on this subject an article by Professor Whitney in the Revue de l'histoire des religions, vol. vi. p. 129, of which a summary is given in the Journal of the American Oriental Society, vol. xi. p. lxxx.

APPENDIX.

APPENDIX.

THE COSMOGRAPHY OF THE ṚIGVEDA.

This appendix will contain a short sketch of the conceptions of the form of the world, the stage on which the cosmological actions are performed, consisting of earth, heaven, and the intermediate spaces. The descriptions of the several parts of the world, in particular of the sky, are so various that it would be folly to attempt to reduce them to uniformity; the object of this sketch is only to supply the reader with a rough indication of the nature of the Vedic ideas on cosmography, which are referred to in the quotations of the essay, with special emphasis on those points where a misconception would be likely to arise.

The earth presented itself to the minds of the poets as above all the broad place (*pṛithivī́, urvī́, mahī́, váraḥ pṛithivyā́ḥ, mahī́ pṛithivī́ várīmabhiḥ*), the extended (*uttānā́*), the boundless (*apārā́*). It is the substratum of the universe (*bhū́mi, kshám, gmā́*); or the place here, simply "this" (*idám*) as opposed to what is yonder. We have mention of the four points of the compass (*e.g.* X. 19. 8.); and the earth thus receives in one passage the epithet "four-cornered" or "four-pointed" (*bhū́miṁ cáturbhṛishṭim* X. 58. 3.). More frequently, however, the point where the speaker stands is represented as one of the regions of the earth, raising the number to five (*páñca pradíçaḥ* IX. 86. 29.); they are enumerated in X. 42. 11. Similarly the inhabitants of the world are described as the five tribes [1] (*páñca kṛishṭáyaḥ*). The earth is depicted in one passage (I. 35. 8.) as containing eight mountains, three continents, and seven streams; the enumeration would seem to be originally mythical, and the corresponding objects sought to suit the previously conceived numbers. The sky has also its seven streams flowing down from the clouds which are its mountains.

The conception of the form of the earth was naturally modified by the coupling of heaven and earth into a single dual conception (*rodasī́, dyā́vā-pṛithivī́, kshoṇī́*). Together they are the two great ones (*mahī́, mākī́, urvī́, varā́*). In one passage they figure as the two halves (II. 27. 15. *ubhā́v árdhau*). From the semi-spherical appearance of the sky they receive the name 'the two bowls turned towards each other' (*samīcīné dhisháṇe*, and apparently *camvā̀* III.

[1] v. s. v. *kṛishṭí*, Pet. Lex.

55. 20.), or they are compared to the wheels at the two ends of an axle (X. 89. 4.). They are equal in size, and both are copies of Indra's greatness (*pratimána*).

Heaven is represented as the realm of shining light (*dív, rocaná, rocanáṁ diváḥ*), as the woven web of light (*vyòman* cf. *uraú pathí vyùte* III. 54. 9.). It is the height (*sánu, pṛishṭhá, vishṭáp*) or the roof of the world supported on high (see Chapter I.). At times we find mention of a firmament above the sky (*divó nắka*) in which the stars are fixed.

More peculiar is the conception of the intermediate space of air, between heaven and earth. The air is not personified to the same extent as heaven and earth, and may therefore be considered a quasi-scientific conception. It is called simply the intermediate space (*antáriksha*) or the *rájas.* The latter word occurs three times in the Ṛigveda in the plural of the dust of the soil; the original sense of the word may have been associated with the fine motes (*márīci*) glittering in the beams of the sun.[1] The *rájas* obstructs the rays of the sun (V. 59. 3.), and can thus be regarded as the cause of darkness, whence the epithet 'black'; when illuminated it is the medium through which the rays are conveyed to the earth (X. 53. 6.). As the dust of the earth receives the rain, so the dust of the air is permeated with

[1] A somewhat similar combination of meanings occurs in the word *purīsha*, cf. *pánthā areṇávaḥ* I. 35. 11., and see K. Z. xxvi. p. 62.

moisture, and hence *rájas* can bear the epithet 'watery' (*aptyám* I. 124. 5., *mádhumat* I. 90. 7.). The limits of the region of the air are said to be indiscoverable.

These three, heaven, earth, and air, are the favourite group of three in the Ṛigveda, underlying all manner of applications of the number. Some whole hymns have no other motive than this continual play on the number (I. 34., III. 56.). According to a common idiom of the Ṛigveda the three may be denoted by any one of the three names; they are even all mentioned together as the three earths, the three heavens, and the three airs;[1] more complication still is occasionally caused by the addition in the singular of one member of the trio, when the three have already been mentioned. The twofold division, again, into heaven and earth, is combined with the threefold division, and thus we have mention of six worlds, or six *rájāṁsi*. These were originally mere freaks of language, but the expressions led to a subsequent real subdivision. In the Ṛigveda we read of an upper, middle and lower heaven (V. 60. 6.); one passage (I. 108. 9, 10.) speaks of an upper, middle and lower earth; the word earth seems in this passage to be used in a loose sense (cf. VII. 104. 11.). In the Atharvaveda, however, the division is clearly defined (A.V. VI. 21. 1.). The triple subdivision is particularly marked in the case of the *rájas*. In the

[1] For a similar manipulation of the numbers compare VII. 33. 7.

highest of the three *rájāṁsi* (*tṛitíye*) are the rain-waters. The two lower regions are within the range of our perception; the third belongs to Vishṇu, whither he stepped with the third of his ascending strides (VII. 99. 1., cf. I. 155. 5.); it is the invisible, mysterious *rájas* (*ádbhutam* X. 105. 7.).[1] More frequently, however, the *rájas* is divided on the twofold principle, the one half belonging to the earth (*pắrthivaṁ rájaḥ*), the other to the sky (*divó rájaḥ*).

Prof. H. Zimmer in his book, 'Altindisches Leben,' p. 357, has alleged the existence of a *rájas* beneath the earth to account for the course of the sun in the night: we will close this sketch with a discussion of his hypothesis. It cannot be doubted that in the majority of cases, where two or three *rájāṁsi* are mentioned, they are conceived as all above the earth. A perfectly clear instance to prove that *pắrthivaṁ rájaḥ* is situated above the earth is I. 81. 5. *ắ paprau pắrthivaṁ rájo badbadhé rocanắ divi*, "he filled the earthly *rájas* and pressed against the sky." The epithet *mádhumat* applied to *pắrthivaṁ rájaḥ* (I. 90. 7.) can scarcely refer to anything under the earth. The presumption is, therefore, that in all cases the same words refer to a *rájas* above the earth. Zimmer refers to three passages, VI. 9. 1.,

[1] The conception of the highest region as hidden above the light, or hidden in impenetrable light, offers an explanation of some passages which have caused difficulty to interpreters, e.g. X. 114. 2. *páreshu gúhyeshu vratéshu* cf. I. 155. 3. and IX. 75. 2.

VII. 80. 1., and V. 81. 4. The first passage reads *áhaç ca krishṇám áhar árjunaṁ ca vi vartete rájasī vedyā́bhiḥ.* Zimmer translates "es durchrollen die lichte und schwarze Tageshälfte offenkundig die beiden Luftkreise." We must compare I. 185. 1. *vi vartete áhanī cakrīyeva,* "day and night revolve like two wheels," i.e. circling round from east to west, the one rising as the other goes down. We are in no way obliged to consider that the progress of either is continued further below the earth. The next passage excludes such an interpretation: *vivartáyantīṁ rájasī sámante āvishkriṇvatī́m bhúvanāni viçvā* (VII. 80. 1.), the dawn "unrolling the two *rájasī,* which border on one another, revealing all things." Here Zimmer remarks, "beide Gebiete stossen aneinander;" the limits, however, coincide just as well if we regard both *rájasī* as narrowing down together towards east and west (cf. V. 47. 3.), or the adjacent borders may be the horizontal plane which separates them. The question is decided by the consideration that only one moment is described, namely, that of daybreak; the dawn is represented as unrolling, unfolding both together, and at the same time as giving light to the world. On the other passage V. 81. 4., *utá rā́trīm ubhayátaḥ párīyase,* Zimmer observes, "die Nacht umwandelt Sūrya von beiden Seiten." The verse is, however, addressed not to Sūrya but to Savitar, who, though in some sense a god of the sun, has a special character as god of the evening. I translate then, "and thou encompassest the night on both sides" (cf. IX. 86. 6).

But if we dismiss the hypothesis of a *rájas* under the earth, how did the poets of the Ṛigveda explain the course of the sun? In one passage an explanation appears to be offered; the words are *ayáṁ cakrám ishaṇat súryasya ny étaçaṁ rīramat sasṛimāṇám | á kṛishṇá īm juhurāṇó jigharti tvacó budhné rájaso asyá yónau* (IV. 17. 14.). Indra stops the chariot of the sun, and, turning it round, flings it into the concealing darkness, apparently the darkness belonging to the night-sky, the way that it came. A similar idea occurs in the Aitareya Brāhmaṇa (3. 4. 44.), where the sun is said to turn round so as to shine downwards in the daytime and upwards in the night. In the same way we are told that it is another *rájas* which accompanies the sun to the east, different from the light with which he rises (X. 37. 3); the light which his horses draw is now bright, now dark (I. 115. 5.), or the path along which his horses travel becomes dark (I. 164. 47.). Such an explanation was, however, inapplicable to the stars, and one poet asks in wonder, "These stars, which are set on high, and appear at night, whither do they go in the daytime?" (I. 24. 10.); and even in the case of the sun a doubt is expressed in the question, "how many suns are there and how many dawns?" (X. 88. 18.)

INDEX OF PASSAGES.

An asterisk is affixed to those passages which are wholly or partially translated, or which form the subject of special comment.

RIGVEDA.

INDEX OF SANSKRIT WORDS.

GENERAL INDEX.

THE HIBBERT LECTURES.

1878.—PROFESSOR MAX MUELLER. Lectures on the Religions of India. 8vo. cloth. 10*s*. 6*d*.

1879.—P. LE PAGE RENOUF. Lectures on the Religion of Ancient Egypt. Second Edition. 8vo. cloth. 10*s*. 6*d*.

1880.—M. ERNEST RENAN. On the Influence of the Institutions, Thought and Culture of Rome on Christianity, and the Development of the Catholic Church. 8vo. cloth. 10*s*. 6*d*.

1881.—DR. T. W. RHYS DAVIDS. Lectures on some Points in the History of Indian Buddhism. 8vo. cloth. 10*s*. 6*d*.

1882.—PROFESSOR KUENEN. Lectures on National Religions and Universal Religions. 8vo. cloth. 10*s*. 6*d*.

1883.—THE REV. CHARLES BEARD. Lectures on the Reformation of the Sixteenth Century in its Relation to Modern Thought and Knowledge. 8vo. cloth. 10*s*. 6*d*.

1884.—PROFESSOR ALBERT REVILLE. Lectures on the Ancient Religions of Mexico and Peru. 8vo. cloth. 10*s*. 6*d*.

1885.—PROFESSOR PFLEIDERER. Lectures on the Influence of the Apostle Paul on the Development of Christianity. 8vo. cloth. 10*s*. 6*d*.

1886.—PROFESSOR RHYS. Lectures on Celtic Heathendom. 8vo. (In the press.)

1887.—PROFESSOR SAYCE. Lectures on the Religion of Ancient Assyria and Babylonia. 8vo. cloth. 10*s*. 6*d*.

Works Published by the Hibbert Trustees.

Illustrations of the History of Mediaeval Thought in the Departments of Theology and Ecclesiastical Politics. By Reginald Lane Poole, M.A., Balliol College, Oxford, Ph.D. Leipzig. 8vo. cloth. 10*s*. 6*d*.

The Objectivity of Truth. By George J. Stokes, B.A., Senior Moderator and Gold Medallist, Trinity College, Dublin; late Hibbert Travelling Scholar. 8vo. cloth. 5*s*.

An Essay on Assyriology. By George Evans, M.A., Hibbert Fellow. With an Assyrian Tablet in Cuneiform Type. 8vo. cloth. 5*s*.

The Development from Kant to Hegel, with Chapters on the Philosophy of Religion. By Andrew Seth, Assistant to the Professor of Logic and Metaphysics, Edinburgh University. 8vo. cloth. 5*s*.

Kantian Ethics and the Ethics of Evolution. A Critical Study by J. Gould Schurman, M.A., D.Sc., Professor of Logic and Metaphysics in Acadia College, Nova Scotia. 8vo. cloth. 5*s*.

The Resurrection of Jesus Christ. An Essay, in Three Chapters. By Reginald W. Macan, Christ Church, Oxford. 8vo. cloth. 5*s*.

WILLIAMS AND NORGATE,
14, HENRIETTA STREET, COVENT GARDEN, LONDON;
AND 20, SOUTH FREDERICK STREET, EDINBURGH.

THEOLOGICAL TRANSLATION FUND LIBRARY.

A Series of Translations by which the best results of recent theological investigations on the Continent, conducted without reference to doctrinal considerations, and with the sole purpose of arriving at truth, will be placed within reach of English readers. Three volumes 8vo. annually for a Guinea Subscription, or a selection of six or more volumes at 7*s*. per vol.

1. Baur (F. C.) Church History of the First Three Centuries. Translated from the Third German Edition. Edited by the Rev. Allan Menzies. 2 vols. 8vo. 21*s*.
2. Baur (F. C.) Paul, the Apostle of Jesus Christ, his Life and Work, his Epistles and Doctrine. A Contribution to a Critical History of Primitive Christianity. Second Edition. By the Rev. Allan Menzies. 2 vols. 21*s*.
3. Bleek's Lectures on the Apocalypse. Edited by the Rev. Dr. S. Davidson. 10*s*. 6*d*.
4. Ewald (H.) Commentary on the Prophets of the Old Testament. Translated by the Rev. J. Frederick Smith. 5 vols. 8vo. Each 10*s*. 6*d*.
5. Ewald (H.) Commentary on the Psalms. Translated by the Rev. E. Johnson, M.A. 2 vols. 8vo. Each 10*s*. 6*d*.
6. Ewald (H.) Commentary of the Book of Job, with Translation by Professor H. Ewald. Translated from the German by the Rev. J. Frederick Smith. 1 vol. 8vo. 10*s*. 6*d*.
7. Hausrath (Professor A.) History of the New Testament Times. The Time of Jesus. By Dr. A. Hausrath, Professor of Theology, Heidelberg. Translated, with the Author's sanction, from the Second German Edition, by the Revs. C. T. Poynting and P. Quenzer. 2 vols. 8vo. 21*s*.
8. Keim (Th.) History of Jesus of Nazara. Considered in its connection with the National Life of Israel, and related in detail. Translated by Arthur Ransom and the Rev. E. M. Geldart. 6 vols. 8vo. Each 10*s*. 6*d*.
9. Kuenen (A.) The Religion of Israel to the Fall of the Jewish State. Translated by A. H. May. 3 vols. 8vo. 31*s*. 6*d*.
10. Pfleiderer (Professor O.) Paulinism: a Contribution to the History of Primitive Christian Theology. Translated by E. Peters. 2 vols. 21*s*.
11. Pfleiderer (Professor O.) The Philosophy of Religion. Translated by the Rev. Alexander Stewart, of Dundee, and the Rev. Allan Menzies. (In 4 vols.) Vol. I. 10*s*. 6*d*. (Vols. II.—IV. in the press.)
12. Protestant Commentary on the New Testament; with General and Special Introductions to the Books, by Lipsius, Holsten, Lang, Pfleiderer, Holtzmann, Hilgenfeld, and others. Translated by the Rev. F. H. Jones. 3 vols. 8vo. 31*s*. 6*d*.
13. Reville (Rev. Dr.) Prolegomena of the History of Religion, with Introduction by Professor Max Müller. 10*s*. 6*d*.
14. Schrader (Professor E.) The Old Testament and the Cuneiform Inscriptions. Translated by the Rev. Owen C. Whitehouse. (In 2 vols.) Vol. I. Map. 10*s*. 6*d*. (Vol. II. in the press.)
15. Zeller (E.) The Acts of the Apostles Critically Examined. To which is prefixed Overbeck's Introduction from De Wette's Handbook. Translated by Joseph Dare. 2 vols. 8vo. 21*s*.

The price of the Works to Subscribers, 7s. per vol.

All new Subscribers may purchase any of the previous volumes at 7*s*. instead of 10*s*. 6*d*. per volume. A selection of six or more volumes may also be had at the Subscribers' price, or 7*s*. per volume.

CATALOGUE

OF

WILLIAMS AND NORGATE'S PUBLICATIONS.

Æschylus. **Agamemnon.** Greek Text revised and translated by John F. Davies, B.A. 8vo, cloth. 3*s.*

Agnostic's Progress, An, from the Known to the Unknown. Crown 8vo, cl. 5*s.*

Ali (Syed Ameer) Life of Mohammed. A Critical Examination of the Life and Teachings of Mohammed, from a Mohammedan Standpoint, including Chapters on Polygamy, Slavery, Moslem Rationalism, Moslem Mysticism, &c. Crown 8vo, cloth. 9*s.*

Alviella (Count Goblet d') The Contemporary Evolution of Religious Thought in England, America and India. Translated by the Rev. J. Moden. 8vo, cloth. 10*s.* 6*d.*

Attwell (Professor H.) Table of Aryan (Indo-European) Languages, showing their Classification and Affinities, with copious Notes; to which is added, Grimm's Law of the Interchange of Mute Consonants, with numerous Illustrations. A Wall Map for the use of Colleges and Lecture-rooms. 2nd Edition. Mounted with rollers. 10*s.*

—— **Table of the Aryan Languages,** with Notes and Illustrations. 4to, boards. 7*s.* 6*d.*

Bannister (Rev. Dr. J.) Glossary of Cornish Names, Ancient and Modern, Local, Family, Personal, 20,000 Celtic and other Names in use in Cornwall. 8vo, cloth. 12*s.*

Baur (F. C.) Church History of the First Three Centuries. Translated from the Third German Edition. Edited by Rev. Allan Menzies. 2 vols. 8vo, cloth. 21*s.*

—— **Paul, the Apostle of Jesus Christ,** his Life and Work, his Epistles and Doctrine. A Contribution to a Critical History of Primitive Christianity. Translated by Rev. A. Menzies. 2 vols. 8vo, cloth. 21*s.*

Bayldon (Rev. G.) Icelandic Grammar. An Elementary Grammar of the Old Norse or Icelandic Language. 8vo, cl. 7*s.* 6*d.*

Beard (Rev. C.) Lectures on the Reformation of the Sixteenth Century in its Relation to Modern Thought and Knowledge. (Hibbert Lectures, 1883.) 8vo, cloth. (Cheap Edition, 4*s.* 6*d.*) 10*s.* 6*d.*

—— **Port Royal,** a Contribution to the History of Religion and Literature in France. 2 vols. 8vo. 12*s.*

Beard (Rev. Dr. J. R.) The Autobiography of Satan. Crown 8vo, cloth. 7*s.* 6*d.*

Bernstein and Kirsch. Syriac Chrestomathy and Lexicon. Chrestomathia Syriaca cum Lexico. 2 vols. in 1. 8vo, cloth. 7*s.* 6*d.*

Bible, translated by Samuel Sharpe, being a Revision of the Authorized English Version. 5th Edition of the Old Testament, 9th Edition of the New Testament. 8vo, roan. 4*s.* 6*d.*

—— vide also Testament.

Bible for Young People. A Critical, Historical, and Moral Handbook to the Old and New Testaments. By Dr. H. Oort and Dr. J. Hooykaas, with the assistance of Dr. Kuenen. Translated from the Dutch by the Rev P. H. Wicksteed. 6 vols. Crown 8vo. 20*s.*

Bleek (F.) Lectures on the Apocalypse. Edited by Dr. S. Davidson. 8vo, cloth. 10*s.* 6*d.*

Bopp (F.) Comparative Grammar of the Sanscrit, Zend, Greek, Latin, Lithuanian, Gothic, German, and Slavonic Languages. Translated by E. B. Eastwick. 4th Edition. 3 vols. 8vo, cloth. 31*s.* 6*d.*

Cobbe (Miss F. Power) The Peak in Darien, and other Inquiries touching Concerns of the Soul and the Body. Crown 8vo, cloth. 7*s.* 6*d.*

—— **A Faithless World.** With Additions and a Preface. 8vo, cloth. 2*s.* 6*d.*

—— **The Duties of Women.** A Course of Lectures delivered in London and Clifton. 2nd Edition. Crown 8vo, cloth. 5*s.*

—— **The Hopes of the Human Race,** Hereafter and Here. Essays on the Life after Death. With a Preface having special reference to Mr. Mill's Essay on Religion. 2nd Edition. Cr. 8vo. 5*s.*

—— **Alone to the Alone.** Prayers for Theists, by several Contributors. 3rd Edition. Crown 8vo, cloth. 5*s.*

—— **Broken Lights.** An Inquiry into the Present Condition and Future Prospects of Religious Faith. 3rd Edition. 5*s.*

—— **Dawning Lights.** An Inquiry concerning the Secular Results of the New Reformation. 8vo, cloth. 5*s.*

—— **Darwinism in Morals,** and (13) other Essays (Religion in Childhood, Unconscious Cerebration, Dreams, the Devil, Auricular Confession, &c. &c.). 8vo, cloth. 5*s.*

Cureton (Dr. W.) History of the Martyrs in Palestine, by Eusebius, in Syriac. Edited and translated. Royal 8vo, cloth. 10*s.* 6*d.*

Dante's Inferno, the Purgatorio, and the Paradiso. Translated into Greek verse by Mussurus Pasha, D.C.L. 3 vols. 8vo, cloth. each 12*s.*

Davids (T. W. Rhys) Lectures on the Origin and Growth of Religion, as illustrated by some Points in the History of Indian Buddhism. (Hibbert Lectures, 1881.) 8vo, cloth. 10*s.* 6*d.*

Day (Dr. F.) The Fishes of Great Britain and Ireland; being a Natural History of such as are known to inhabit the Seas and Fresh Waters of the British Isles. 179 Plates. 2 vols. imp. 8vo, cloth. £5. 15*s.* 6*d.*

Delitzsch (Professor F. R.) The Hebrew Language viewed in the Light of Assyrian Research. Crown 8vo, cloth. 4*s.*

Dipavamsa, the: a Buddhist Historical Record in the Pali Language. Edited, with an English Translation, by Dr. H. Oldenberg. 8vo, cloth. 21*s.*

Echoes of Holy Thoughts: arranged as Private Meditations before a First Communion. 2nd Edition, with a Preface by Rev. J. Hamilton Thom. Printed with red lines. Fcap. 8vo, cloth. 2*s.* 6*d.*

Engelhardt (C.) Denmark in the Early Iron Age. Illustrated by recent Discoveries in the Peat-Mosses of Slesvig. 33 Plates (giving representations of upwards of a thousand objects), Maps, and numerous other Illustrations on wood. 4to, cloth. 31*s.* 6*d.*

Evans (George) An Essay on Assyriology. With 4to Tables of Assyrian Inscriptions. 8vo, cloth. 5*s.*

Ewald's (Dr. H.) Commentary on the Prophets of the Old Testament. Translated by the Rev. J. F. Smith. Complete in 5 vols. Vol. I. General Introduction, Yoel, Amos, Hosea and

Zakharya 9—11. Vol. II. Yesaya, Obadya and Mikha. Vol. III. Nahûm, Ssephanya, Habaqqûq, Zachârya, Yéremya. Vol. IV. Hezekiel, Yesaya xl.—lxvi. Vol. V. and last, Haggai, Zakharya, Malaki, Jona, Baruc, Daniel, Appendix and Index. 8vo, cloth. 5 vols. Each 10*s.* 6*d.*

—— **Commentary on the Psalms.** Translated by the Rev. E. Johnson, M.A. 2 vols. 8vo, cloth. Each 10*s.* 6*d.*

—— **Commentary on the Book of Job,** with Translation. Translated from the German by the Rev. J. Frederick Smith. 8vo, cloth. 10*s.* 6*d.*

Frankfurter (Dr. O.) Handbook of Pali; being an Elementary Grammar, a Chrestomathy, and a Glossary. 8vo, cloth. 16*s.*

Fuerst (Dr. Jul.) Hebrew and Chaldee Lexicon to the Old Testament. 4th Edition, improved and enlarged. Translated by Rev. Dr. Samuel Davidson. Royal 8vo, cloth. 21*s.*

—— Kept also half-bound morocco. 26*s.*

Gill (C.) The Evolution of Christianity. 2nd Edition. With Dissertations in Answer to Criticism. 8vo, cloth. 12*s.*

Goldschmidt (H. E.) German Poetry; with the English Versions of the best Translators. Poems of Goethe, Schiller, Freiligrath, Bürger, Heine, Uhland, Körner, &c. &c. Translated by Carlyle, Anster, Blackie, Sir Th. Martin, Shelley, Lord Ellesmere, Lord Lytton, Coleridge, Longfellow, Edgar Bowring, Garnett, &c. 8vo, cloth. 5*s.*

Gostwick (J.) and R. Harrison. Outlines of German Literature. Dedicated to Thos. Carlyle. New Edition. 8vo. 10*s.*

Gould (Rev. S. Baring) Lost and Hostile Gospels. An Account of the Toledoth Jesher, two Hebrew Gospels circulating in the Middle Ages, and extant Fragments of the Gospels of the first Three Centuries of Petrine and Pauline Origin. Crown 8vo, cloth. 7*s.* 6*d.*

Hanson (Sir R. D.) The Apostle Paul and the Preaching of Christianity in the Primitive Church. By Sir R. D. Hanson, Chief Justice of South Australia, Author of "The Jesus of History," &c. 8vo, cloth. (Published at 12*s.*) 7*s.* 6*d.*

Hardy (R. Spence) Manual of Buddhism in its Modern Development. Translated from Cingalese MSS. 2nd Edition, with a complete Index and Glossary. 8vo, cloth. 21*s.*

—— **Eastern [Buddhist] Monachism;** an Account of the Origin, Laws, Discipline, Sacred Writings, &c. &c. of the Order of Mendicants founded by Gotama Buddha. 8vo, cloth. 12*s.*

Hariri. The Assemblies of Al Hariri. Translated from the Arabic, with an Introduction and Notes. Vol. I. Introduction and the first Twenty-six Assemblies. By T. Chenery, Esq. 8vo, cloth. 10*s.*

Hausrath. History of the New Testament Times. The Time of Jesus. By Dr. A. Hausrath, Professor of Theology, Heidelberg. Translated by the Revds. C. T. Poynting and P. Quenzer. 2 vols. 8vo, cloth. 21*s.*

Hemans (Chas. I.) Historic and Monumental Rome. A Handbook for the Students of Classical and Christian Antiquities in the Italian Capital. Crown 8vo, cloth. 10*s.* 6*d.*

—— **History of Mediæval Christianity and** Sacred Art in Italy (A.D. 900—1500). 2 vols. Crown 8vo, cloth. 18*s.*

Jones (Rev. R. Crompton) Hymns of Duty and Faith, selected and arranged. 2nd Edition. Crown 8vo, cloth. 3*s.* 6*d.*

Keim's History of Jesus of Nazara. Considered in its connection with the National Life of Israel, and related in detail. Vol. I. Introduction, Survey of Sources, Sacred and Political Groundwork, Religious Groundwork.

Vol. II. The Sacred Youth, Self-recognition, Decision. Vol. III. The First Preaching, the Works of Jesus, the Disciples, and Apostolic Mission. Vol. IV. Conflicts and Disillusions, Strengthened Self-confidence, Last Efforts in Galilee, Signs of the approaching Fall, Recognition of the Messiah. Vol. V. The Messianic Progress to Jerusalem, The Entry into Jerusalem, The Decisive Struggle, The Farewell, The Last Supper. Vol. VI. The Messianic Death at Jerusalem, Burial and Resurrection, The Messiah's Place in History, Indices. 8vo, cloth. Each 10*s.* 6*d.*

Knighton (W.) Struggles for Life. By William Knighton, LL.D., Vice-President of the Royal Society of Literature; Author of "The History of Ceylon," "Forest Life in Ceylon," &c. &c. Cloth. 10*s.* 6*d.*

Kuenen (Dr. A.) The Religion of Israel to the Fall of the Jewish State. Translated by A. H. May. 3 vols. 8vo. 31*s.* 6*d.*

—— Lectures on National Religions and Universal Religions. (Hibbert Lectures, 1882.) 8vo, cloth. 10*s.* 6*d.*

Laing and Huxley. Pre-Historic Remains of Caithness. By Samuel Laing, Esq., with Notes on the Human Remains by Th. H. Huxley, F.R.S. 150 Engravings. 8vo, cloth. 9*s.*

Lane (E. W.) Arabic-English Lexicon, derived from the best and most copious Eastern Sources. Vols. I. to VII. (to be completed in 8 vols.). Royal 4to. Each 25*s.*

—— Vol. VIII. Fasc. 1. Edited by Stanley Lane-Poole. 4to. 6*s.*

Latham (Dr. R. G.) Two Dissertations on the Hamlet of Saxo-Grammaticus and of Shakespear. 8vo. 5*s.*

Laurie (Professor Simon) Ethica; or the Ethics of Reason. By Scotus Novanticus. 8vo, cloth. 6*s.*

Laurie (Professor Simon) Metaphysica Nova et Vetusta: a Return to Dualism. 8vo, cloth. 6*s.*

Lepsius (C. R.) Standard Alphabet for reducing Unwritten Languages and Foreign Graphic Systems to a Uniform Orthography in European Letters. 2nd Edition. 8vo, cloth. 3*s.*

Lyall (C. J., M.A., C.I.E.) Ancient Arabian Poetry, chiefly præ Islamic; Translations, with an Introduction and Notes. Foolscap 4to, cloth. 10*s.* 6*d.*

Macan (R. W.) The Resurrection of Jesus Christ. An Essay in three Chapters. Published for the Hibbert Trustees. 8vo, cloth. 5*s.*

Mackay (R. W.) Sketch of the Rise and Progress of Christianity. 8vo, cloth. (Published at 10*s.* 6*d.*) 6*s.*

Macvicar (Rev. Dr. J. G.) A Sketch of a Philosophy. Part I. Mind: its Powers and Capacities, and its Relation to Matter; II. Matter and Molecular Morphology: the Elemental Synthesis; III. The Chemistry of Natural Substances; IV. Biology and Theodicy. 4 Parts. 8vo. 25*s.* 6*d.*

Massey (Gerald) A Book of the Beginnings. Containing an Attempt to recover and reconstitute the lost Origines of the Myths and Mysteries, Types and Symbols, Religion and Language, with Egypt for the Mouthpiece and Africa as the Birthplace. 2 vols. Imperial 8vo, cloth. 30*s.*

—— **The Natural Genesis;** or Part the Second of "A Book of the Beginnings." 2 vols. Imp. 8vo, cloth. 30*s.*

Milinda Panho, the. Being Dialogues between King Milinda and the Buddhist Sage Nāgasena. The Pali Text, edited by V. Trenckner. 8vo. 21*s.*

—— vide also Pali Miscellany.

Mind, a Quarterly Review of Psychology and Philosophy. Nos. 1—40. 1876-85. 8vo, each 3*s.* Annual Subscription, post free, 12*s.*

Müller (Professor Max) Lectures on the Origin and Growth of Religion, as illustrated by the Religions of India. (Hibbert Lectures, 1878.) 8vo, cloth. 10*s.* 6*d.*

Nibelungenlied. The Fall of the Nibelungers, otherwise the Book of Kriemhild. An English Translation by W. N. Lettsom. Crown 8vo, cloth. 7*s.* 6*d.*

Norris (E.) Assyrian Dictionary. Intended to further the Study of the Cuneiform Inscriptions of Assyria and Babylonia. Vols. I. to III. 4to, cloth. Each 28*s.*

O'Curry (Eug.) Lectures on the Social Life, Manners and Civilization of the People of Ancient Erinn. Edited, with an Introduction, by Dr. W. K. Sullivan. Numerous Wood Engravings of Arms, Ornaments, &c. 3 vols. 8vo. 42*s.*

Oldenberg (Prof. H.) Buddha, his Life, his Doctrine, and his Order. Translated by Dr. Wm. Hoey, B.C.S. 8vo. 18*s.*

—— vide Vinaya Pitakam.

Pali Miscellany, by V. Trenckner. Part I. The Introductory Part of the Milinda Panho, with an English Translation and Notes. 8vo. 4*s.*

Peill (Rev. George) The Threefold Basis of Universal Restitution. Crown 8vo, cloth. 3*s.*

Perrin (R. S.) Religion of Philosophy, The; or the Unification of Knowledge. A Comparison of the chief Philosophical and Religious Systems of the World. 8vo, cloth. 16*s.*

Pfleiderer (O.) Paulinism: a Contribution to the History of Primitive Christian Theology. Translated by E. Peters. 2 vols. 8vo. 21*s.*

—— **Philosophy of Religion** on the Basis of its History. I. History of the Philosophy of Religion from Spinoza to the present Day. Vol. I. Spinoza to Schleiermacher. Translated by the Rev. Allan Menzies and the Rev. Alex. Stewart, of Dundee. 8vo. 10*s.* 6*d.*

Pfleiderer (O.) Lectures on the Influence of the Apostle Paul on the Development of Christianity. (Hibbert Lectures, 1885.) 8vo, cloth. 10*s.* 6*d.*

Platonis Philebus, with Introduction, Notes and Appendix; together with a Critical Letter on the "Laws" of Plato, and a Chapter of Palæographical Remarks, by the Rev. Dr. Chas. Badham, D.D. 2nd Edition, enlarged. 8vo, cloth. 4*s.*

—— **Euthydemus et Laches,** with Critical Notes and "Epistola critica" to the Senate of the Leyden University, by the Rev. C. Badham, D.D. 8vo, cl. 4*s.*

—— **Convivium (Symposium),** with Critical Notes and an Epistola (de Platonis Legibus) to Dr. Thompson, Master of Trinity College, Cambridge, by the Rev. C. Badham, D.D. 8vo, cloth. 4*s.*

Poole (Reg. L.) Illustrations of the History of Medieval Thought in the Departments of Theology and Ecclesiastical Politics. (Printed for the Hibbert Trustees.) 1884. 8vo, cloth. 10*s.* 6*d.*

Pratt (Dr. Henry) New Aspects of Life and Religion. 440 pp. Crown 8vo, cloth. 7*s.* 6*d.*

Protestant Commentary, A Short, on the Books of the New Testament: with general and special Introductions. Edited by Professors P. W. Schmidt and F. von Holzendorff. Translated from the Third German Edition, by the Rev. F. H. Jones, B.A. 3 vols. 8vo, cloth. Each 10*s.* 6*d.*

Quarry (Rev. J.) Genesis and its Authorship. Two Dissertations. 2nd Edition, with Notice of Animadversions of the Bishop of Natal. 8vo. 12*s.*

Reliquiæ Aquitanicæ; being Contributions to the Archæology and Palæontology of Périgord and the adjoining Provinces of Southern France. By Lartet and Christy. Edited by T. Rupert Jones, F.R.S., F.G.S. 87 Plates, 3 Maps, and 130 Wood Engravings. Royal 4to, cloth. £3. 3*s.*

Renan (E.) On the Influence of the Institutions, Thought and Culture of Rome on Christianity and the Development of the Catholic Church. (Hibbert Lectures, 1880.) 8vo, cloth. (Cheap Edition, 2*s.* 6*d.*) 10*s.* 6*d.*

Renouf (P. le Page) Lectures on the Origin and Growth of Religion as illustrated by the Religion of Ancient Egypt. (Hibbert Lectures, 1879.) 2nd Edition. 8vo, cloth. 10*s.* 6*d.*

Reville (Dr. Alb.) Prolegomena of the History of Religions. With an Introduction by Professor F. Max Müller. 8vo, cloth. 10*s.* 6*d.*

—— **On the Native Religions of Mexico and Peru.** Translated by the Rev. P. H. Wicksteed. (Hibbert Lectures, 1884.) 8vo, cl. 10*s.* 6*d.*

—— **The Song of Songs,** commonly called the Song of Solomon, or the Canticle. Crown 8vo, cloth. 1*s.* 6*d.*

Sadi. The Gulistan (Rose-Garden). Persian Text, with Vocabulary by Johnson. Royal 8vo, cloth. 15*s.*

Saltus (E.) Anatomy of Negation. Crown 8vo, cloth. 7*s.* 6*d.*

Samuelson (James) Views of the Deity, Traditional and Scientific: a Contribution to the Study of Theological Science. Crown 8vo, cloth. 4*s.* 6*d.*

Savage (M. J.) Beliefs about the Bible. By the Rev. M. J. Savage, of the Unity Church, Boston, Mass. 8vo, cloth. 7*s.* 6*d.*

Schmidt (A.) Shakespeare Lexicon. A complete Dictionary of all the English Words, Phrases, and Constructions in the Works of the Poet. 2 vols. Imp. 8vo, 28*s.*; cloth, 31*s.* 6*d.*

Schrader (Professor E.) The Cuneiform Inscriptions and the Old Testament. Translated from the second Enlarged Edition, with Additions by the Author, by the Rev. Owen C. Whitehouse, M.A. (In 2 vols.) Vol. I. With a Map. 8vo, cloth. 10*s.* 6*d.*

Schurman (J. G.) Kantian Ethics and the Ethics of Evolution. A Critical Study. (Published by the Hibbert Trustees.) 8vo, cloth. 5*s.*

Seth (A.) The Development from Kant to Hegel, with Chapters on the Philosophy of Religion. (Published by the Hibbert Trustees.) 8vo, cloth. 5*s.*

Sharpe (Samuel) History of the Hebrew Nation and its Literature. With an Appendix on the Hebrew Chronology. 4th Edition, 487 pp. 8vo, cl. 7*s.* 6*d.*

—— **The Decree of Canopus,** in Hieroglyphics and Greek, with Translations and an Explanation of their Hieroglyphical Characters. 16 Plates. 8vo, cloth. 7*s.* 6*d.*

—— **Hebrew Inscriptions** from the Valleys between Egypt and Mount Sinai, in their Original Characters, with Translations and an Alphabet. 2 Parts. 20 Plates. 8vo, cloth. 7*s.* 6*d.*

—— vide also Bible, and Testament.

Smith (Arthur M.) A System of Political Economy. 2nd Edition. 502 pp. Crown 8vo, cloth. 7*s.* 6*d.*

Smith (Rev. J. F.) Studies in Religion under German Masters. Essays on Herder, Goethe, Lessing, Frank, and Lang. Crown 8vo, cloth. 5*s.*

—— vide Ewald's Prophets and Job.

Socin (A.) Arabic Grammar. Paradigms, Literature, Chrestomathy, and Glossary. Translated into English. Crown 8vo, cloth. 7*s.* 6*d.*

Sophocles. The Greek Text critically revised, with the aid of MSS., newly collated and explained. By Rev. F. H. M. Blaydes. I. Philoctetes. II. Trachiniæ. III. Electra. IV. Ajax. 8vo, cloth. Each 6*s.*

Spencer (Herbert) First Principles. 5th Thousand, with an Appendix. 8vo. 16*s.*

—— **The Principles of Biology.** 2 vols. 8vo. 34*s.*

Spencer (Herbert) The Principles of Psychology. 4th Thousand. 2 vols. 8vo. 36*s*.

—— **The Principles of Sociology.** Vol. I. 21*s*.

—— **Ceremonial Institutions.** (Principles of Sociology, Vol. II. Part 1.) 8vo. 7*s*.

—— **Political Institutions.** (Principles of Sociology, Vol. II. Part 2.) 8vo. 12*s*.

—— **Ecclesiastical Institutions.** 2nd Edition. 8vo, cloth. 5*s*.

—— **The Data of Ethics.** Being the First Portion of the Principles of Ethics. 8vo, cloth. 8*s*.

—— **The Study of Sociology.** Library Edition (being the 9th), with a Postscript. 8vo, cloth. 10*s*. 6*d*.

—— **Education:** Intellectual, Moral, and Physical. 8vo, cloth. 6*s*.

—— The same, cheaper Edition, 4th Thousand. 12mo, cloth. 2*s*. 6*d*.

—— **Essays:** Scientific, Political, and Speculative. (Being the First and Second Series re-arranged, and containing an additional Essay.) 2 vols. 4th Thousand. 8vo, cloth. 16*s*.

—— **Essays.** (Third Series.) Including the Classification of the Sciences. 3rd Edition. 8vo. 8*s*.

—— **Descriptive Sociology,** or Groups of Sociological Facts. Compiled and abstracted by Professor D. Duncan, of Madras, Dr. Richard Sheppig, and James Collier. Folio, boards. No. 1. English, 18*s*. No. 2. Ancient American Races, 16*s*. No. 3. Lowest Races, Negritto Races, Polynesians, 18*s*. No. 4. African Races, 16*s*. No. 5. Asiatic Races, 18*s*. No. 6. American Races, 18*s*. No. 7. Hebrews and Phœnicians, 21*s*. No. 8. The French Civilization, 30*s*.

Spinoza. Four Essays by Professors Land, Van Vloten, and Kuno Fischer, and by E. Renan. Edited by Professor Knight, of St. Andrews. Crown 8vo, cloth. 5*s*.

Stephens (George) Old Northern Runic Monuments of Scandinavia and England, now first collected and deciphered. Numerous Engravings on Wood and 15 Plates. 3 vols. Each 50*s*.

Stokes (Geo. J.) The Objectivity of Truth. 8vo, cloth. 5*s*.

Stokes (Whitley) Old Irish Glossaries. Cormac's Glossary. O'Davoran's Glossary. A Glossary to the Calendar of Oingus the Culdee. Edited, with an Introduction and Index. 8vo, cloth. 10*s*. 6*d*.

—— **Middle-Breton Hours.** Edited, with a Translation and Glossary. 8vo, boards. 6*s*.

—— **The Creation of the World.** A Mystery in Ancient Cornish. Edited, with Translations and Notes. 8vo, cloth. 6*s*.

Strack (H. L.) Hebrew Grammar. Paradigms, Literature, Chrestomathy, and Glossary. Crown 8vo, cloth. 4*s*. 6*d*.

Strauss (Dr. D. F.) Life of Jesus for the People. The Authorized English Edition. 2 vols. 8vo, cloth. 24*s*.

Sullivan (W. K.) Celtic Studies, from the German of Dr. Hermann Ebel, with an Introduction on the Roots, Stems and Derivatives, and on Case-endings of Nouns in the Indo-European Languages. 8vo, cloth. 10*s*.

Taine (H.) English Positivism. A Study of John Stuart Mill. Translated by T. D. Haye. Crown 8vo, cloth. 3*s*.

Talmud of Jerusalem. Translated for the first time into English by Dr. Moses Schwab, of the Bibliothèque Nationale, Paris. Vol. I. The Treatise of Berakhoth (Blessings). Foolscap 4to. 9*s*.

Tayler (Rev. John James) An Attempt to ascertain the Character of the Fourth Gospel, especially in its relation to the first Three. 2nd Edition. 8vo, cl. 5*s*.

Testament, The New. Translated by S. Sharpe, Author of "The History of Egypt," &c. 14th Thousand. Fcap. 8vo, cloth. 1*s.* 6*d.*

Thoughts (365) for Every Day in the Year. Selected from the Writings of Spiritually-minded Persons. By the Author of "Visiting my Relations." Printed with red lines. Crown 8vo, cl. 2*s.* 6*d.*

Turpie (Dr. D. McC.) The Old Testament in the New. The Quotations from the Old Testament in the New classified according to their Agreement with or Variation from the Original: the various Readings and Versions of the Passages, Critical Notes. Royal 8vo, cloth. 12*s.*

—— **Manual of the Chaldee Language:** containing Grammar of the Biblical Chaldee and of the Targums, a Chrestomathy, Selections from the Targums, with a Vocabulary. Square 8vo, cl. 7*s.*

Vinaya Pitakam: one of the principal Buddhist Holy Scriptures. Edited in Pali by Dr. H. Oldenberg. In 5 vols. 8vo. Vol. I. The Mahâvagga. Vol. II. The Cullavagga. Vol. III. The Suttavibhanga, I. (Pârâjika, Samghâdisesa, Aniyata Nissaggiya). Vol. IV. The Suttavibhanga, II. (Mahavibhanga, Bhikkunivibhanga). 8vo. Each 21*s.*

Williams (Rev. Dr. Rowland) The Hebrew Prophets, during the Assyrian and Babylonian Empires. Translated afresh from the Original, with regard to the Anglican Version, with Illustrations for English Readers. 2 vols. 8vo, cloth. 22*s.* 6*d.*

—— **Psalms and Litanies,** Counsels and Collects, for Devout Persons. Fcap. 4to, cloth extra. 12*s.* 6*d.*

—— **Broadchalke Sermon-Essays** on Nature, Mediation, Atonement, Absolution, &c. Crown 8vo, cloth. 7*s.* 6*d.*

Wright (G. H. B.) The Book of Job. A new critically revised Translation, with Essays on Scansion, Date, &c. 8vo, cloth. 6*s.*

Zeller (Dr. E.) The Contents and Origin of the Acts of the Apostles critically investigated. Preceded by Dr. Fr. Overbeck's Introduction to the Acts of the Apostles from De Wette's Handbook. Translated by Joseph Dare. 2 vols. 8vo, cloth. 21*s.*

WILLIAMS & NORGATE have published the following Catalogues of their Stock.

1. Classical Catalogue. Greek and Latin Classics.
2. Theological Catalogue. Including Philosophy and Metaphysics.
3. French Catalogue. General Literature, History, Travels, &c.
4. German Catalogue. General Literature.
 * Map Catalogue. Foreign Maps and Atlases.
5. Linguistic Catalogue. European Languages.
 * Italian Catalogue.
 * Spanish Catalogue.
6. Oriental Catalogue. Oriental Languages and Literature.
7. Medical Catalogue. Medicine, Surgery, &c.
8. Natural History Catalogue. Zoology, Botany, Geology, Palæontology.
9. Natural Science Catalogue. Mathematics, Astronomy, Physics, Mechanics, Chemistry, &c.
10. Art Catalogue. Architecture, Painting, Sculpture and Engraving. Books illustrated by Artists.
11. School Catalogue. Elementary Books, Maps, &c.